Laughter in a Time of Turmoil

Laughter in a Time of Turmoil

Humor as a Spiritual Practice

Richard P. Olson

WIPF & STOCK · Eugene, Oregon

LAUGHTER IN A TIME OF TURMOIL
Humor as a Spiritual Practice

Wipf & Stock
An Imprint of Wipf and Stock Publishers
199 W. 8th Ave., Suite 3
Eugene, OR 97401
www.wipfandstock.com

ISBN 13: 978-61097-866-8
Manufactured in the U.S.A.

Grateful acknowledgement is given to Ave Maria Press for permission to reprint a prayer by Edward Hays from his book *Pray All Ways* (copyright 1981, 2007); to the Joyful Newsletter, http://www.joyfulnewsletter.com for permission to quote "The Clown's Prayer" by Cal Samra; to Penguin Group (USA) Inc. for permission to quote from *The Courage to Laugh* by Allen Klein (copyright 1998); and to Continuum Books for permission to quote from *A Time to Laugh: The Religion of Humor* by Donald Capps (copyright 2005).

Dedicated to the memory of three zestful and witty friends / mentors—
Leland (Lee) Regier
Dave Johnson
Donna Beth Noren Blythe

"I thank my God in all my remembrance of you . . . thankful for your partnership in the gospel from the first day until now . . . again I will say, Rejoice."

—Phil 1:3, 5,: 4:4 (RSV)

Contents

Foreword

WHEN I RECEIVED THE manuscript of the book you are now holding in your hands I scanned the table of contents and saw right away that there are nine chapters. The analogy of a baseball game entered my head and it wouldn't let go. In fact, I found myself humming the tune of the familiar baseball song "Take Me Out to the Ballgame" and it was all I could do to resist the urge to go out and buy me some peanuts and Cracker Jacks.

As I began reading, the analogy proved to be even more inspired than it had a right to be. In chapter one, Richard Olson introduces his "mentor / models" who taught him the spiritual practice of smiling, laughter, and humor. It was easy to translate "mentor" to "coach," and to think of chapter one as the first inning of a baseball game as the players, with their coaches' inspiring words still ringing in their ears, take the field and say to themselves and to one another, "Let's go out there and win this game!" From Lee Regier Richard learned that many parts of ministry are play—and fun to do—but, as every baseball player knows, some aspects of the game are work and not at all fun to do. For Lee, the aspects of ministry that were not fun were pastoral calls on people he cared deeply about who were suffering (see chapter six) and church administration (see chapter eight). From Dave Johnson—who was one of the best softball pitchers in his county—Richard learned the value of humor from a lay person who had a serious physical handicap. As he notes, Dave accomplished so much in his life and his humor was the door through which he walked to accomplish them. From Donna Beth Noren Blythe—a truly blithe spirit—he learned the love of teasing, heckling and repartee.

And, of course, although coaches may claim that the raw material they have to work with is terrible and the worst they've seen in years, they know in their hearts that their players have a great deal of natural talent, oftentimes greater than their own, and this is also the sense we get from chapter one, that Richard already had the natural talent to play the game and that his coaches were mainly there to encourage him to use it. This, of course, raises the question why some are naturally endowed with a sense of humor and others have to work hard to acquire it (but this question anticipates chapter 5).

The next two chapters focus on the varieties of humor and the good things that humor can do for us. These chapters are analogous to the second and third innings of a baseball game—the teams are getting to know something about their opponents' strengths and weaknesses and trying, if possible, to get an early lead while knowing, of course, that the lead may change several times before the game is ended. This is also the time when the folks in the stands are settling into their seats, drinking cokes and eating popcorn, and even chatting a bit with their companions as they watch the game. But most of all, they are saying to themselves, "I hope this will be a good game, whoever wins." And this is precisely what these chapters also convey: Humor (or, at least, most humor) is a good thing, especially when we don't view it in terms of winners and losers, for with humor, everyone can feel good about having played or watched the game. And this being so, we can see how Richard is laying the foundation for his claim that humor may be numbered among the spiritual practices for the healing and sustaining of ministry. In effect, these chapters make the case for knowledge about humor. And although one may be able to enjoy a baseball game without knowing the slightest thing about baseball and why the players are doing what they are doing, it's hard to get "serious" about the game without a working knowledge of it. In this sense, Richard is advising us to get serious about humor, but not so serious that we take the fun out of it. Chapters four and five provide the biblical and theological foundations for the spiritual practice of humor. Chapter four shows that there's a lot of humor in the Bible, and maybe we would have discovered this on our own if we had been allowed to think that God, its ostensible author, has a great sense of humor.[1] That God has a great sense of humor is the main point of chapter five. It provides the theological underpinnings for experiencing God by listening for the laughter that emanates from heaven. But chapter five also suggests that we need an ethics of humor, one builds on evidence

1. We also learn in this chapter that baseball itself is biblical because the book of Genesis reports that "In the big inning . . . Eve stole first and Adam stole second." This may lead us to wonder why God forgot to tell Adam (the guy in charge) that in the divine scheme of things, boys play baseball, girls play tennis.

presented in chapter three that humor can be good for us (hence, it performs a moral function). Ethics involves reasoned reflection on moral issues and values, and it is here that Richard suggests that the purpose of the book is to work in two directions—not only to broaden understanding of the variety of types and benefits of humor practice but also to encourage thoughtful examination and abandoning of unhelpful humor practice. A lot of humor is good for the soul, but some of it isn't, and ethical reflection involves learning to separate the wheat from the chaff. These chapters, then, are not unlike the fourth and fifth innings of a baseball game as these are the innings when the inspiring words of the coaches and the momentum afforded by enthusiasm begins to wear off and the players need to attend to the fundamentals—to show that they are well grounded, more substance than style.

And this brings us to chapters six, seven, and eight, which focus on the particularities of ministry and how the spiritual practice of humor may open up otherwise unforeseen or unimagined opportunities, options, and benefits which might otherwise go unseen, untapped, or unexploited.

These are the innings in baseball when players on both teams take reasonable chances and risks in hopes of shaking things loose and making things happen that might not otherwise happen. Thus, in chapter six on humor and pastoral care, Olson discusses, among other things, the positive uses of surprise (think of the runner on first base who rounds second and then heads for third on a shallow fly to right field), or making use of ambiguity (think here of the runner on third base who rattles the pitcher by taking an unusually long lead off as if he intends to steal home).

In chapter seven Richard considers the positive uses of humor in preaching, leading worship, and Christian Education and small groups, and emphasizes the value of playfulness. The seventh inning is about that point in a game when both teams (call them the Baptist Wildcats and the Presbyterian Bulldogs) are most likely to forget that baseball, after all, is only a game: A starting pitcher who has been replaced with a reliever may walk dejectedly off the field and throw his glove into the dugout, or a batter called out on strikes may begin hurling curse words at the home plate umpire. Richard suggests that preaching and worship are occasions for lightening up, and invokes the theology presented in chapter five of God as having a great sense of humor in support. When preaching gets dull and worship gets boring, it's time for a seventh inning stretch, and humor is there to stretch us.

In chapter eight Richard tackles[2] church administration—what his mentor friend Lee Regier considered one of the least fun aspects of ministry. The eighth inning is the one when the team that is behind has the most difficulty keeping its spirits up and the team that is ahead prays that someone won't do something stupid and blow their comfortable lead. This is also the inning when disgusted fans pack up their belongings and head for the parking lots to get ahead of the crowd and beat the traffic. But Richard is saying that it is precisely at times like this when a little humor can do a world of good, whether it comes from the mascot who wags his tail at the disconsolate pitcher, or from the umpire who points to the sky, as if to suggest that only God has perfect vision.

And this brings us to chapter nine on identifying and developing a new spiritual practice—in this case, the spiritual practice of humor. Here the baseball analogy is almost too obvious, leading some to suspect that whoever first proposed the idea of "spiritual practices" was thinking of whatever competitive sport was popular at the time, for sports are like learning to play the piano—its takes practice, practice, and more practice, and the more one practices, the more one doubts the claim that practice makes perfect. But what Richard has done here in this book is to show through many illustrations and anecdotes that humor is a spiritual practice that one engages in with others. To be sure, we can laugh to ourselves about something that strikes us funny, but humor loves company, for after all, humor is a team sport.

At one time or another in our lives, many of us considered trying out for a place on a team but decided, for one reason or another, to let it go. Maybe we thought we didn't have enough natural talent. Maybe we thought the other players would wonder what we were doing there or what made us think we might be good enough to make the team. But with the spiritual practice of humor, it's no cliché to say that everyone can play, and the more the merrier! And as Richard demonstrates in this book, it helps a lot to have a coach who knows his way around the bases.

Donald Capps
Princeton Theological Seminary

2. This unintended football allusion illustrates what happens to our minds when baseball and football seasons overlap.

Preface

For the last few years I have been playing with the idea of humor—mainly the ability to laugh at oneself—as an important resource to keep one strong and resilient when providing care and giving leadership. At the same time I was reading and teaching on spiritual formation. This led to the topic of spiritual practices, and the deeper I went, the more it seemed to me that humor ought to be considered one of those practices.

Eventually I became convinced that this is indeed so—that humor is indeed a spiritual practice—and so now I want to convince you. I am persuaded that a healthy dose of humor, play, and lively, supportive friends can help one heal when bruised, and can provide the needed rest / recuperation when one is fatigued, burned out, weary and stressed. I truly believe that humor is a spiritual possibility to uphold those who take on heavy responsibilities for the Christian cause.

To convince you, I will introduce you to three of my unforgettable friends. Then I will walk around the topic of humor from conceptual, biblical, theological, practical application, and spiritual practices perspectives. In all of this, I will hold a number of possibilities before you.

I hope you enjoy this read. Quite probably you will enjoy it even more if you find a group of people and read / reflect together, swap stories, and compare your own experiences, wisdom, and insights with those in this book. There are discussion questions at the end of each chapter to help you get started on such conversations.

If you experience even a little laughter, support, relief, renewal or insight for your life and service as a result of reading this book, I will be twice blessed. I've already had a blast ministering to me while creating it. Enjoy and Rejoice.

Acknowledgments

I am in debt to many persons in bringing this project to fruition. I acknowledge that debt and express my thanks to the following:

The families of Lee Regier, Dave Johnson, and Donna Beth Noren Blythe, for permission to tell their stories and providing additional information.

A number of friends who filled out a questionnaire, and / or submitted to an interview, and / or swapped thoughts on this topic. You will see most of their names when I mention their contribution.

My colleagues on the faculty, administration and staff at Central Baptist Theological Seminary. They allowed me to share some of this during faculty enrichment, and challenged hard enough to make it better. Thanks also for excellent library support services.

Donald Capps for generous encouragement and friendship to a stranger and for writing the Foreword.

Jennifer Harris Dault for doing the copy editing and preparing the manuscript for typesetter.

The staff of Wipf and Stock that saw this project through to its conclusion.

The generous response of participants at gatherings and retreats where I have presented some of this material. They both let me know what was funny and what was not!

Introduction

What I Didn't Know I Knew

I WAS HOPING TO be kind and supportive. What I received was more than I gave.

A pastor friend had invited me for beverages and conversation at a local coffee house, and I thought I knew why. For a while we caught up on each other's lives, as good friends do. And then, our talk took a serious turn.

She spoke of pain and struggle. Though she had a clear vision for the church, this vision was not unanimously accepted. Her gifts in ministry were taken for granted by some and demeaned by others. Several families—including a few significant leaders—had left. She had faced some hard decisions; her choices were criticized and rejected by sizeable minorities in the congregation.

She asked me to compare my experience with hers. Were my visions and dreams for the church usually accepted? No, not often—certainly not quickly. Did members fail to recognize my gifts and hope for different styles of Bible interpretation and preaching? Yes, quite a number did. Had folks left the congregations I served in disapproval of my ministry? Some did. Did I have to make hard decisions that were not liked or widely supported? Yes.

We were aware that the churches we had served, for all of their marvelous qualities, were not easy places to do ministry. If there are any such places of comfortable service, neither of us had found them. Rather, the atmosphere in which she does parish ministry is even more brittle and harsh than it was for me. These are times of great turmoil for many who serve and love the church. (I retired from parish ministry fourteen years ago. In active semi-retirement I now teach pastoral theology in a seminary.)

She asked what wisdom or advice I had to give her. I had none to offer, only encouragement, companionship, and support. This didn't seem to be much, and I expressed regret that I had nothing more.

"That's OK," she said, "It's nice to talk with someone who's been through what I am going through and is still smiling." We said good-bye shortly after that.

"Still smiling," That phrase came back to me again and again. She picked up on something central to me. Indeed, she had named the truth I knew but didn't know I knew.

Those two words stirred life reflection. I recalled that smiles and laughter have indeed been an important part of my Christian walk. As a child and youth, I delighted in stories and laughter during worship or Sunday School. I particularly liked it when my father-minister would tell stories about his childhood. The fun of youth groups and especially church camps (in the beautiful Black Hills of South Dakota) was rich indeed.

In college I forged lifelong friendships with a group of folks who teased each other unmercifully, heckled any of us who risked leadership, enjoyed practical jokes, and endlessly discovered new shenanigans that kept us from taking things (including our education and our empty pockets) too seriously. We found something to laugh about at every occasion. In seminary I was drawn to friends with a similar love of play, fun, and humor.

When I began parish ministry—though I missed the supportive hospitality and fun of those friends—I tried in my own small ways to bring the qualities of joyous enthusiasm, excitement, play, and liveliness to the congregations I served. However, ministry is not easy. There are times of tragedy and of conflict, resistance, and rejection. In some of these times,

THE FUN IN THE ENGLISH LANGUAGE

1. Atheism is a non-prophet organization.
2. What if there were no hypothetical questions?
3. Is there another word for synonym?
4. Where do forest rangers go to "get away from it all?"
5. What do you do when you see an endangered animal eating an endangered plant?
6. How is it possible to have a civil war?
7. Can an atheist get insurance against acts of God? (Excerpt from circulated email)

my smile and chuckle would falter and become tentative. Sometimes it entirely disappeared. I am grateful that was only temporary. Then, one way or another, the joy would return.

Over the years, I have made many wonderful friends who have enriched my life and expanded my humor experience. Phone calls, emails, visits, and reunions revive and nourish this precious gift for me. I seem to buy or be given all sorts of books on this subject. From time to time, I am asked to provide classes, workshops, or retreats on story and humor in ministry.

My friend's "still smiling" comment drew me back to these memories. As regards this humor practice, I am fortunate to have good genes, a great family heritage, and many hilarious and playful friends. But, even beyond these wonderful gifts to me, deep down I know that this is vital to who I am and what I do. Further, I have chosen to develop, nurture, and experiment with it.

As one whose temperament is quite sensitive to strain, criticism, rejection, abandonment, and conflict, humor has two absolutely vital contributions: it helps to heal me when I am hurting; and it helps to sustain and renew me when I am weary, burned out, or close to giving up.

Of course, there are other aspects as well—people enjoy humor from the pulpit and other events; however, much more important than making others laugh is that *we* who minister laugh, regularly and often. While humor as a tool of ministry is helpful (and we'll talk about that), even more significant is humor as a vital source of renewal for us as Christian leaders and ministers.

Therefore, I believe that humor deserves much more attention, specific encouragement, and calling forth than is usually given it. Books on stress management in ministry may mention humor as a coping device; however, it is usually done in a minor "by the way" sort of manner. They devote a paragraph, a page, or at most a brief chapter to the subject. Humor in service and ministry, I am convinced, is much more essential than that.

What is this more central place?

Humor deserves to be considered a *spiritual practice.*

What do I mean—humor as a *spiritual practice*? At least these:

- An intentional, conscious choice and thus an action, a repeated action,
- A part of me to attend, to explore, to nourish, to develop consistently,

- The decision to be engaged in this often, regularly, consistently, whether I feel like it or not—to "practice" it,
- A curiosity about the range of humor possibilities and openness to stretch my own personal repertoire of humor in which I engage.

These, in turn, may lead to further development, including these:

- An inquiry into the connection between humor and biblical-theological teachings, and an application of some of those concepts to humor,
- A recognition not only of humor's possibilities, but its limitations, and the other spiritual practices with which it needs to be intertwined,
- And, at the same time, a sensitivity to dark humor and to the potential misuse or abuse of humor.

A bit of clarification may be useful. This suggestion of humor as a spiritual practice is in the context of the wider discussions of roads to spiritual maturity. Various writers use two different terms to describe the various ways one can grow. Some speak of disciplines (the more traditional term) and some speak of practices (in some of the more recent discussions). I could speak of humor as a spiritual discipline (consider that if it is helpful) but choose to use the term "practice" instead.

Of course, no one discipline/practice suffices for a growthful Christian life; rather a combination is needed. I will discuss disciplines (Richard Foster) and practices (the Valparaiso Project) in more detail in chapter 9, argue for the inclusion of humor on those lists of disciplines/practices (neither includes humor at the present time), and examine where it fits. While I have put that discussion at the end, feel free to read chapter 9 now if you would like a clearer idea of where we are going.

Also, it will be helpful to clarify the use of the key words "humor," "comedy," and "comic."

Humor has a range of meaning, for example:

- Something that arouses amusement or laughter,
- The capacity for recognizing, reacting to, or expressing something which is funny,
- A mood or frame of mind, to be in "good humor."

And then, there are two additional nuanced definitions which may be sometimes especially important to a church leader:

- To let a person have one's own way for the sake of peace and quiet,
- To keep someone in a good temper.[3]

> A learned minister "of another denomination, meaning to be slightly sarcastic, once said to [Peter] Cartwright (nineteenth century Methodist frontier preacher) 'How is it that you have no doctors of divinity in your denomination?'
>
> "'Our divinity is not sick and don't need doctoring,' said the sturdy backwoodsman."—Frontispiece in Doug Adams, *Humor in the American Pulpit*.

Comedy also has a range of meanings:

- A drama which seeks to please by amusing, and which always has a happy ending,
- A real life situation that suggests such drama,
- The laughter-provoking element in some situation, whether real or imagined.

Closely related, definitions of *comic* also have a range of meanings:

- Funny, amusing,
- A part in a comedy,
- An amusing person,
- A magazine of drawings
- The humorous element in life or art[4]

While both comedy and comic can refer to specific literary forms, for the most part I will engage all three terms—humor, comedy, and comic—in the broad definitions of them and use them interchangeably. When, on a few occasions, I refer to comedy as a literary form, I will make that clear. Conrad Hyers once noted, "In the comic spirit, humor is the spirit, comedy the form; and laughter is its overt expression."[5]

And so, as we explore the deeper significance of sustaining humor and laughter in times of turmoil, here is the plan for this book:

3. *The New Webster's Dictionary of the English Language*, 472.
4. *Ibid.* 195–96.
5. Hyers, *Holy Laughter: Essays on Religion in the Comic Spirit*, 6.

1. Meet some special people with spiritual gifts of humor; then consider the vast varieties of types of humor; and note the contributions of humor in the areas of physical health, psychological benefits, and religious-spiritual renewal.
2. Examine Scripture for the humor within it, and then, develop a basic theology and ethic of humor.
3. Describe the possible enrichment humor offers—in pastoral care, when the people of God gather, and when giving church and community leadership (including in the midst of conflict and criticism).
4. Consider Christian disciplines/practices and humor's rightful place among these; and also explore how to grow in this practice.

Some of this will be of interest to any who enjoy a good laugh and would like to know a bit more about humor (chapters 1–3). More of it will speak to those who see themselves as spiritual or religious and who long for more zest, joy, and growth in their lives (chapters 4, 5, and 9). Still other portions will mostly interest people rendering care giving and ministry, whether clergy or lay (chapters 6–8).

To do this, I will carry on a dialogue between my personal experience and that of my generous friends, a lot of books/journals/Web sites, and a survey I sent out to some clergy folk.

Some books yield insights on humor but are totally humorless themselves. There are also books of humor that provide laughs but little insight. My attempt will be to walk the middle road between those two extremes. I hope some of the things offered here are enjoyable and call for a smile or chuckle. But even more, this is an invitation to an open door of renewed and sustainable service and ministry.

In chapter 1, experience the stories of three people who opened this door for me.

QUESTIONS FOR PERSONAL AND GROUP REFLECTION

1. Recall a time when humor was helpful in performing some act of ministry. Was it helpful for caregiver, care receiver, or both? Was the humor intentional or accidental? What did the humor contribute to the experience?

2. Recall a time when humor was helpful to you personally. Did you initiate the humor or did someone else? How did you feel before the humor? How did you feel afterward?
3. As you look out at the church of today, what areas are in need of some gentle, healing humor?
4. As you look out at the world, what areas are in need of a humorous perspective?
5. In this chapter I shared a bit of my "humor history." That is a starting point in developing/strengthening this practice. Take a look at yours. When were laughter and play the easiest and most frequent in your life? When decreased or gone? Where are you now?
6. I confessed that my friend's chance remark awakened me to awareness of this spiritual practice of humor that was already important in my life of service. What have you discovered about this spiritual practice of humor in your life?
7. If you are reading this book as part of a discussion or support group, what hopes do you have—for the group? From the book? What agreements and covenants would you like with the group? (If you are not already in a group, can you think of one or more friends with whom you would like to read/discuss this exploration?)

1

Two Amigos and an Amiga

(My Mentors / Models Who Taught Me This Practice)

Joy is the most infallible sign of the presence of God.

—attributed to Teilhard de Chardin

In an early scene of the musical *Sound of Music* the nuns of the abbey are pondering in song "How Do We Solve a Problem like Maria," who, in so many ways is disruptive and just doesn't fit in. One nun, however, offers a different perspective. She sings, "I'd like to say a word on her behalf—Maria makes me laugh!"

I am so enriched and blessed because of those in my life who—like Maria—made me laugh. Even more, they modeled humor as a spiritual practice for me. Here are my recollections of three of them.[1]

LEE REGIER

Comedians are innately programmed to pick up oddities like mispronounced words, upside-down books on a shelf, and generally undetectable mistakes in everyday life . . . I think it was Jack Benny who once said, 'A comic says funny things, but a comedian says things funny.' I guess I'd fall into that latter grouping.

—Bob Newhart[2]

1. These stories are told with the permission of, as well as the participation and contribution of surviving family members.

2. Newhart, *I Shouldn't Even Be Doing This*, 5–6.

Lee was one of the two closest friends I ever had. We met when we were both teenagers, but we didn't get off to a very good start at that first meeting. Each of us had come to our denomination's state youth convention without a roommate, and so we were assigned to stay together. Both preacher's kids, both lonely, we talked about a lot of things into the night. As he later recognized, "The church of my childhood was much too serious, somber, and angry." He reflected that background and seemed to me to be self-righteous and judgmental. After that convention, I remember thinking, "Lee is probably a pretty good Christian guy, but no one that I could have any fun with." Nevertheless, we occasionally wrote each other in the months following.

The next fall we were classmates in a small church related college in our home state (Sioux Falls College, now University of Sioux Falls) and became close friends over the next four years. Very quickly I saw another side to him as he became the campus clown.

His sense of play and adventure would help us find ways to entertain ourselves with the very few funds we had. He fell in and out of love several times in those years, not without a good bit of laughter about his perils of romance (sometimes more than one at the same time). He would often lure me away from my books late at night to drive downtown for a cheap hamburger, or if we were even more broke, just drive around a little, looking for excitement.

In the summer after our junior year, he married Barbara (at very least the second Barbara he had dated) which increased his joy in living—a romance that continued to the end of his life. Their little apartment became the scene for great hospitality and good fun over that last year of college.

After graduation, we went to seminaries on opposite coasts—he at Berkeley, I in the Boston area. Ron Erickson, who became a seminary friend during their Berkeley days, remembers Lee during that time as loving fast cars, country music, exaggerating almost anything and spending hours in the seminary's sound studio doing church versions of "Bob and Ray" (a radio comedy team from the 1950s) routines.

When we finished our seminary educations, we both began pastorates back in our home state, and again we found ways to spend time together. In a few years, we both moved to different states. But whether we were geographically close or not, we kept finding ways to keep our friendship alive. He would call me and visit at length, back when long distance calls were expensive and considered a luxury. The reasons would be varied—to get some ideas or illustrations for a sermon, to explore an issue, to ask advice, but more often to tell his latest story or freshest joke.

We would bring each other to our churches for some leadership or enrichment event. And while we faithfully did what was promised, the more basic reason was to be together to share laughs, delight, and play. We knew that if we spent as much as three days together, at some point we would laugh ourselves into helplessness. The knees would buckle under us. Probably if you asked us ten minutes later what was so funny, we couldn't have told you.

Once, when he was coming for an activity at my church, my then junior high daughter Julie asked if she could come with me to pick him up at the airport. "Why do you want to come, honey?" I asked. She responded, "Because you guys are nuts." She was not the only one who noticed. People in my congregations told me that they saw me in a new light when Lee and I were together. He brought out my inner playful child like no one else ever has. There was wonder, delight, mischievousness, pranks, play, and much laughter when we were together.

Lee and Barb bought many Bob Newhart and Smothers Brothers records. We would listen to them time and again. Then we would begin improvising Newhart- or Smothers-type skits about various frustrating circumstances at church.

He had the knack for seeing humor where others had missed it. Once when he was visiting, we picked up my wife, Mary Ann—who was seven months pregnant—from her sewing class that met in the local union hall. As we stopped to get her, he burst out laughing. Only he had noticed this expectant mother was standing in the doorway under the sign "Labor Temple." He would pick up on a person's manner of expressing things, the way a policeman was directing traffic, someone's mistimed belch or flatulence, and usually—but not always in an appropriate place—get the giggles himself until others were laughing with him.

Once when I visited him, the only thing he could find to do that night was a professional wrestling match, and so we went. I must admit that if I had gone by myself, I would only have seen the phoniness, the fake moves, and the deceit. He saw it as high drama, wonderful showmanship, great fun, and a chance to shout, boo, jeer, laugh—and learn a few things about how to put on an event. We had a great time and relived it into the night until sleep overtook us.

His love of play and insisting on play were qualities that kept him going. Always a highly competitive athlete, he rarely let the competition overshadow the fun of the game. For years in his ministry he played in a table tennis league every Tuesday night and noted that if he didn't do that, something happened to him. He also planned a date night with Barbara every week, sometimes including their beloved daughter Deborah. Carefully planned and preserved time for activities he loved with people he treasured fed his spirit and kept him alive in ministry.

This carried over into his work as minister. In the only formal interview I ever did with him, he told me, "Some parts of ministry are play to me. Preaching is play. Teaching a class of interested people is play . . . I'm glad to wake up each morning and know I have a job to go to, a place to be. I think it's a privilege to stand where Christ should stand, to be where Christ should be, whether it is at a communion table, pulpit, baptismal, funeral, hospital, or nursing home. I represent a purpose, a power, something worthwhile. I just love it—for the most part."[3]

One of the things he loved most was being involved with people in the crises and emergencies of their lives. He was known to follow an ambulance or fire truck to see what was going on and to be of help if needed. One of his friends said it accurately, "For relaxation, Lee goes to a riot."

The parts that were not play for him included administration and calls on people he cared deeply about who were suffering badly. He also found it was not play to need to sit and write something. (His sermons, mostly a lively oral form were derived from much reflection/study and notes to remind him where to go next.) He felt that when he did write, it sounded "dumb." This was one of his frustrations. He would have loved to tell me the important discoveries of his heart and mind and have me write them down for him.

In his ministry, he found ways to do the "not fun" parts of ministry efficiently and quickly, or delegated. In this way he not only had a better time, he concentrated on what he did well.

Lee was a wonderful resource of encouragement to my ministry. In my low moments or times of anger at some perceived injustice that had

3. This and following quotes of the interview are found in "Making Time for Play" by Barbara and Leland Regier in *The Stained Glass Fishbowl*, 49–61.

been inflicted on me, I would call him. He'd listen for a little while. Then I would hear a suppressed guffaw on the other end of the line, "They did what, Ole[4]?" And he would likely launch into yet a new variation of one of our Bob Newhart-wannabe routines. Within minutes I'd be laughing with him, and before I hung up, I'd be calmer and have more perspective on what was going on.

In that interview I mentioned, he reflected on the spiritual significance of the changes from his religiously restrictive childhood. "In experimenting with my playfulness, I rediscovered Christ. Up to that time I had missed the Christ who said, 'I have come that you might have life and have it more abundantly.' That is the Christ that inspires my life and ministry.

"I am reminded of Jesus' word, 'You are like children in the market place. We play for you and you won't dance. We play a dirge for you and you won't mourn.' He was asking 'Why won't you respond to life as it is?' I was determined that life was too short to be so mad all the time. I guess I'm selfish. I can give a lot to ministry if I get back a lot. Whether it's nine o'clock at night or 2 a.m., I want to have some laughs, I want to have a good time. It's self-protection. Why be miserable? The rabbis used to say it is wrong not to enjoy the good life, including all that God has made for us."

Barb added, "There's a verse in the Psalms that we laugh about a great deal. 'This is the day the Lord has made. We will rejoice and be glad in it.' It's like a command. You *will* rejoice! We like that. It's been important in our lives."

There was a time when Lee called me with a piece of personal news that both pleased and embarrassed him. The seminary he had attended and he taught field education courses where (in addition to his pastorate), was going to confer an honorary Doctor of Divinity degree on him. He was embarrassed because honorary degrees were one of the things we'd poke fun at all our lives. I assured him his was well deserved and I would come if I could. I did that, as did two other lifelong friends, Ron and Marjorie Erickson.

What a time we had! Lee and Barb met us at the airport with limousine and chauffer so the party could begin at the moment of our arrival. (My suitcase didn't arrive with my flight. In Lee's presence, this inconve-

4. My college nickname.

nience became part of the fun. He later regaled the group with how the luggage man dressed me down for my negativism about this.)

We laughed, ate, and sang into the night each of the evenings we were there. Those folks really knew how to play and celebrate. One night we even had our own folk singer. We then stood proudly with Lee as he was honored for his significant service in ministry and in the training of ministers.

I was a bit shocked at his ashen complexion. We had some frank discussions about health in which he admitted that some of his problems were worsening. He also said that we had not been keeping closely enough in touch, and that we should talk each week. So we did make contact by phone almost every week for the next twelve weeks. Then a call came from Barb saying that Lee had died that morning. He was fifty-six. We had been friends for nearly forty years.

For years afterward, I would pick up the phone with my "sad, mad, or glad" news only to realize I couldn't call and tell him. As time goes on, I have tried to integrate into my life what he used to instill in me when we were together. I think it's going pretty well.

How he would have loved to collaborate with me on this book project! Finally, he would have been able to tell me his ideas and have me write them down. Though we can't do that, I am sure that my memory of his playful wisdom will inform me time and again as I proceed in this project. Without a doubt, he has a prominent place among my mentors of the spiritual practice of humor, laughter, and play.

DAVE JOHNSON

Humour, I think is responsible for more important human advances than physics, medicine, or any other science. It teaches us to see things in proportion.

—George Mikes[5]

To appreciate Dave Johnson's humor, you have to know something of his life before I met him. He had been born in a Swedish-speaking home in a small town in northern Wisconsin. At age six when he went to school, he was expected to speak English, which he could not do. Out of

5. quoted in Klein, *The Healing Power of Humor*, 3.

this trauma—and perhaps other reasons—Dave developed a stuttering handicap that would be with him for the rest of his life.

At the same time, Dave had many gifts. He was bright and a good student—pulled As and Bs without even studying. In addition, he was one of the best softball pitchers in his county.

In one way at least, his stuttering proved to be a blessing. His high school principal contacted a vocational rehabilitation counselor to talk with Dave. This person determined that because of this difficulty, Dave was entitled to scholarship help. With this proffered aid, he became the very first of his family to go to college, one of only three in his whole town to go for any kind of further education. He enrolled in the huge University of Wisconsin, hundreds of miles from his little home town.

For a time, he floundered there. The huge impersonality of the university and the search for a major that was right were overwhelming. A good math and science student, he tried chemical engineering and discovered that was not for him. He also explored his artistic gifts in art courses, but that didn't pan out either. He was drawn to Christian ministry but knew that his speech problem precluded that profession. For a time he developed shingles out of his homesickness, uncertainty, pressure, and depression.

In time, he discovered the Baptist Student Center, which was, among other things, a small shared residential community. Here was a much more comfortable place with compatible people and a campus minister with broad vision. In this setting, Dave began to grow into campus life. However, his restless search for the right major and vocation was sometimes expressed in rebellion, wisecracks, pranks, and other shenanigans in his community.

One year in a house decorating competition for the university's homecoming celebration, Dave and his friends put a toilet commode on the roof of the flat front porch of the house with a big sign, "We'll Flush Northwestern." Though tame by today's standards, the student ministry board was not pleased. The campus minister almost lost his job for refusing to take it down, stating that if the students had thought it inappropriate, they would not have done it.

At another time, the cook had to be gone and Dave volunteered to fix an evening meal. His innovation was to use food coloring and dye the mashed potatoes green, the peas red, and other foods similar exotic colors. He insisted no taste of any food was altered. Still most of it went uneaten.

An attractive high school student, Mary Bond, would stop by the center to see friends once in a while. On occasion she would say she thought she was being followed, possibly stalked, and she would be much more comfortable if someone would walk her home. Dave served as this escort from time to time. A friendship and then romance evolved from these walks. Whenever this story was told, Dave would always refer to the "alleged" stalker, pointing out that he never saw such a person.

Mary came to college the next year, and they continued to date. She recalled, "At first I went out with Dave just for laughs. As I got to know him better, I was struck by the great idealism of his life. He was convinced you must make your life count for something. Over and again, he'd ask, 'Where do I fit? What does God want me to do with my life?'" They married some years later.

A significant event in Dave's life was a student trip to Chicago that his campus minister arranged. There they saw the famous Hull-House, some lesser known Christian centers, the Urban League and movements supporting civil rights. The next summer, he took part in a "Students in Industry" project and learned more of a caring response to pressing social problems. These experiences connected to Dave in a deep way. Here was a form of ministry he could do. Out of these, he began to discern his calling.

He changed his major to social work with a sense of peace and conviction that this was right vocation for him. In time he gained his Master of Social Work degree as well. His career led to the Corrections system in Wisconsin, where he was on the staff of a reformatory for a number of years. Then he was selected to be part of the founding team of a brand new medium security prison with an emphasis on rehabilitation.

By then, he was married with two young children. However, there was to be another severe barrier on the way to this new chapter in his career. At less than thirty years of age, he had a severe heart attack. For weeks his life hung in the balance. It was uncertain whether he would live or die.

At the turning point of this health crisis, Dave had a profound experience/vision. He was aware of being in a hospital bed in a room with a window and billowing curtains (There were no such curtains in his actual hospital room.). The curtains were waving in a strong breeze, and there was light coming through the window. The light became brighter and brighter, and his bed began moving toward the light, as if drawn like a magnet. He felt eager to go to the light.

In time, the light slowly dimmed, and the bed began to recede away from it. He recalled that though he dearly loved his wife and children and his work, he was disappointed when this happened. For he realized it meant he would not have whatever experience the light offered at that time.

I met Dave when he had continued recovery at home and had been able to go back to work. They were new to the community and the church where I was called to be minister, at Beaver Dam in central Wisconsin. At that time, he was still weak with limited energy and often fatigued. Still, he had a great zest for life—quite aware of its shortness and the greater glory to be revealed. He loved and was proud of his wife and family, and he was thrilled at the opportunity in his work.

Dave was also a faithful and helpful church member, one who brought his zany humor with him to church activities. His continuing stuttering handicap was no barrier to his humor; indeed it heightened the anticipation of what was coming.

I must say that it was an adventure when Dave came by to greet me after worship on Sunday morning. Rather than the bland and kindly things most folks said to their minister at that time, it would be something else. When I preached on "Left Handed Men," he came by and wordlessly shook hands,—left handed. Another time, when we had been studying Keith Miller's *Taste of New Wine*, he told me, "I need another copy of *The Drinking Man's Guide* to give to a friend." Most Sundays, he would distort the point of my sermon so completely that I would know he understood it.

His self-humor about his own stuttering was unrelenting.

> A young engineer was leaving the office for the day when he found the CEO standing in front of a shredder with a piece of paper in his hand.
>
> "Listen," said the CEO, "this is a very sensitive and important document and my secretary is not here. Can you make this thing work?"
>
> "Certainly," said the young engineer. He turned his machine on, inserted the paper, and pressed the start button.
>
> "Excellent, excellent!" said the CEO as his paper disappeared inside the machine, "I just need one copy." (Excerpt, circulated email)

For example, "D-Dick, if you ever run out of something to say fifteen minutes early, just ask me to lead in a word of prayer." "I w-would have been a minister except for one thing—I was bad on offerings." Once, when we were eating at their home and someone came to the door, he told them, "I'm sorry to be so slow answering the doorbell. I was saying grace and G-god is one of my hardest words."

At times he would aim his humor at his family who seemed to love to be included in it. "I l-love my job so much that next time I marry, I'll marry for money, so if necessary, I can work for nothing." He also mildly threatened that when Mary turned forty he would have to trade her in for two twenty-year-olds. Whereupon she got off one of her best lines, "But dear, I don't know if you are wired for 220." Once when we were all in the same car driving somewhere, with perfectly straight face, he consistently mixed up the names of the farm animals he and his child saw out the window—stirring a lively and amusing exchange between them.

His colleagues in the prison told me that his humor—particularly his self-humor—was an asset in his work with the inmates. One colleague told me, "The inmates think they got a pretty bum rap. Dave has an obvious handicap, but he is sharp. He can't be conned, and yet he is understanding. He makes his handicap work for him. He is funny about it." Said another co-worker, "He, in a show of strength, laughs at himself. Bob Hope has his nose, Martha Rae has her mouth, and Dave Johnson has his speech. Though some inmates react negatively initially, soon they come to hold him in high regard as they see the way he is able to live with his difficulty."

Dave even brought humor into his anger. Once he was complaining to me about a fellow church member, an insurance agent, who called and insisted that they were somehow obligated to buy insurance from him. Dave in his weakened post heart attack condition: "It made me so mad, that I wanted to buy a million dollar policy and then run up and down the stairs, just to collect."

Then as now, small group life was being emphasized as a means to personal and church renewal. Ministers were advised to get every member into a small group. I tried that with this little Wisconsin church of about 100 members, but I succeeded in getting only one group together. The good news was that it included both Dave and Mary and Donna Beth (the next person I will mention) and her husband John. I don't know how well we succeeded at helping people experience the depth and renewal of which the small group literature spoke. I only know that on the evenings when Dave and Donna Beth started playing off each other, we laughed until the tears rolled down our faces.

I remember one night especially. We'd had our closing prayer, but then Bernadine, our hostess, raised one more question, "I'd like your help on something. When I get up in the morning, I like to do cleaning and other housework in my bathrobe, and not take my own bath and dress for the day until late in the morning. But I would be so embarrassed if the Lord came and I were still in my bathrobe. What do you think I should do?" For a few moments all of us sat speechless. We liked each other a lot, but many of us did not think in these terms and did not know what to say. Finally, Dave spoke up, "Well, B-bernadean, I think you should have your house in order!"

Dave's humor did not forsake him even when great grief came. In her late forties, Mary—who had always lived so healthily—was discovered to have lung cancer which they knew was terminal. They called me to share this tragic news, (I was then in Colorado) and Mary had a request. When she died, would I come to be with the family and conduct her funeral?

I could not immediately answer. Ministerial ethics and etiquette mandated that there needed to be contact, permission, and invitation by the local ministers before a former pastor could participate. I made those contacts, explained the circumstances, and received the invitation I needed.

And so I called Mary and Dave to tell them I would come and to have the difficult conversation of letting Mary tell me what she wanted at her own funeral. Dave and Mary were both on phones at their end of the line.

Mary began thinking about who should participate in the service. There was that kindly fundamentalist minister down the street who would stop by and pray with her. And, there was a former pastor who lived in the area who would phone from time to time. The list went on and on. Finally Dave interrupted, "Mary, this is no time to be meeting your social obligations! Besides, I'm the one who is going have to put up with all those characters." I'm sure we smiled on both ends of the line and then went on to a simpler and essential plan for that time.

When Mary died, the faith and laughter were present as we recalled a wonderful person, a much-too-short life well-lived with care and love, and her amusement/tolerance of Dave's frequent teasing, heckling, playful antics.

Dave had received much medical attention to his weakened heart, including open heart surgery. However, a few years after Mary's death, Dave also died. Again his family called, and again I journeyed to stand with them, to remember in worship and gratitude this great-hearted person who had touched not only me but many others so deeply.

Dave was a person with deep faith, great love, lively and steady commitment. He accomplished so much in serving those in prison, as a family member, as a church leader. More often than not, his humor was the door through which he walked to accomplish those significant things.

DONNA BETH NOREN BLYTHE

If you can find humor in anything, you can survive it.

—Bill Cosby[6]

Donna Beth loved to tell the story of the first time we met. It was the early 60s. My family and I had come to Beaver Dam to begin our pastorate there. The Blythes (John was chaplain at a local college prep academy), members of the church, would provide an evening meal for us, the new ministerial couple, and our two small children the first evening we arrived.

And so after an exhausting five hundred mile drive to a new community, the new clergy family made their way to this gracious meal. However, it all turned sour. Donna Beth had prepared roast chicken for them. This minister sometimes had thought that in his former rural pastorate he was being paid in chickens. Further, he had grown up in a parsonage, where often, the pay or the gifts would be all manner of fowl—geese, ducks, turkey, pheasant, and chicken. He was completely satiated on fowl and heartily disliked it. He hated chicken but with a forced smile sat down and forced down a few bites of it on his first night in a new city.

6. Quoted by Klein, *Healing Power of Humor*, 3.

At least that was how Donna Beth told it. Actually it was a nice meal and warm welcome. I tolerate chicken, not hate it. But as Donna Beth would often say, "Never let the truth get in the way of a good story."

We quickly became close couple friends with much in common. Our children were similar in age to theirs and so there was good company all around. John had attended the same eastern seminary as I did (Andover Newton Theological School), graduating four years ahead of me. Though we had never met at the seminary, we had had the same professors and both knew people in the classes between us. This led to much reminiscing and storytelling. One time Donna Beth asked, "Do you know John Drummond?" Without thinking, I blurted out, "No, but I hate his guts." She asked why. I told her that during seminary I had followed him as part-time youth minister in a suburban church as my field education assignment. For the entire time, the senior minister, Rev. Murphy, compared me unfavorably to John—how organized he was, how well he planned things, how wonderfully the youth and their families responded to him.

A year or so after that conversation, we were at a seminary reunion at a national church gathering. With a twinkle, Donna Beth waved me over to meet someone with whom she was visiting. "Dick, this is John Drummond. Tell him!" A bit embarrassed, my first words to him were, "John, I hate your guts." He looked surprised. When I told him why, he laughed and said that all his time there, Rev. Murphy compared him unfavorably to Joe Lincoln who had preceded him. We enjoyed getting to know each other. Donna Beth even more enjoyed stirring things up and making a little trouble—by no means the only time.

> Bill Geist: "Stopping for the night in rural Kansas, I asked the motel desk clerk if he can recommend the best place in town for dinner. He scratches his head, thinks about it for a while, and says slowly, 'Well . . . I'd have to say the Texaco, 'cuz the Shell don't have no microwave.'" (Bill Geist, 146.)

She loved to tease, heckle, and engage in repartee. John recalls a time when they had just come with their new baby to be on staff of a church with Bob Towner, in Madison, Wisconsin. They came to the Towner's home, and Donna Beth was bathing the baby in the kitchen sink. Bob, who loved to tease Donna Beth, came in from a meeting, took one look at the new baby and commented, "What a cute little small mouth bass." Bob was quite a good singer, and Donna Beth came right back with, "Better than a large mouth bass!"

I recall another of those little exchanges. It took place in the book store of a convention gathering. John and Donna Beth were looking at the new books. One I wrote about remarriage was on display. Pretending not to see me, Donna Beth told John, "Oh John, don't bother buying Dick's book. He writes book after book and always says the same thing. But he charges more each time a new one comes out." And so on in the same vein. When she finished, I came up to them to her pretended surprise. "John," I told him. "Buy it, even if it is a lot of money. It's worth it. It will help you pick out your next wife." She laughed the loudest and gave me a big grin as if to say, "Good one, Dick." She didn't seem to care who "won" such verbal contests, and there was no meanness in them. She did it only for the fun of engagement and play.

A minister's spouse, a choir member, leader, and soloist with a lovely voice, a lifelong faithful church person, still she had little patience with overwhelming super piety or the wordiness of many ministers. This impatience sometimes expressed itself in iconoclastic and irreverent humor. I don't remember how it started, but an expression of this was how we came to customarily greet each other. We would give each other a little hug and whisper into the other's ear, "How the hell are you?" Though they moved from Beaver Dam much too soon and we would see them only occasionally at denominational meetings, I could always count on that greeting. When, from time to time, a stranger would come up to me with a greeting from a friend with those words, I knew exactly who sent it.

Donna Beth grew up in Nebraska, in a family that thoroughly enjoyed humor and practical jokes. She bought into these qualities and carried them with her all her life.

She would tell how she and John got together. They were both freshmen in beginning speech class in a small denominational college (Ottawa University in Kansas), but they had not yet spoken to each other. In this class, each person had to give a brief speech introducing oneself. When John did his speech, he mentioned his birthday, December 11. Donna Beth recounted, "That was my birthday, too! And, as you can see, he's a gorgeous hunk of man. So when I stood up to give my speech, I coyly mentioned that 'someone' had spoken of a birth date of December

11. I added that is my birthday, too. After class he spoke to me and asked me if that was really my birthday. We started talking, and we've been talking ever since."

Indeed. They married, had five children, and served together in a variety of capacities. They advocated for a broad and ecumenical church as well as for social justice / political stands on behalf of the oppressed and underdog. These were not often popular positions in the places they served. Humor, hospitality, enjoyment of people, love of stories carried them where more severe confrontation would not have. As one of her pastors pointed out, she got away with saying some controversial and outrageous things, because she always said them with a smile.

Donna Beth had multiple sclerosis, which, over the years, restricted her mobility. First she had to walk with a cane. Then she was confined to wheel chair. However, even with these difficulties, they made their way to a remarkable variety of venues—vacations, concerts and plays, church gatherings and social occasions. If there was self pity, the rest of us never heard of it.

If I knew they were going to be at a social gathering, I went hoping to sit at their table. But I would have to get there early. Many friends wanted the same thing, knowing that story and laughter would flow freely.

Donna Beth died a few years ago. Her memorial service was a triumphant celebration of her and her joy of living. The church was filled to overflowing. There was beautiful music. A soloist sang "Come Unto Me"— the same song from Handel's Messiah that she had sung all four years with her college choir. The minister recalled the word with which she always greeted him—"Yes."

Her fine adult children shared brief tributes. All of them were lovely, but we walked out chuckling at what son Chris said. He began, apologetically stopped to answer his cell phone, and went on, in the style of a Bob Newhart routine. It went something like this. "Hello. Mom? You're calling from heaven? And you're using weekend minutes? Well, dad would be proud of that. So, mom, what is heaven like? . . . Mostly Baptists and democrats? And women? Always a jokester aren't you? You're not kidding? What do you think of the service so far? OK, more music, less talking. You always loved the music, didn't you? I remember how you always used to time dad's sermons. And you always let him know how long he'd talked,—to the minute. Oh, I'll tell Marcus (the church's pastor) that you're watching him too. Mom, there's an awful lot of your friends, family, and admirers here today. What's that? You wish you could be here with us? You are and you always will be. We love you." We roared. Donna Beth would have loved it. We went out smiling and comforted that such a person had been a part of our lives.

AND SO—

You may be feeling badly for me and wondering, "Are all your best friends dead?" No, I still have friends with whom I laugh, and you will hear comments from some of them before we finish this conversation. I continue to be drawn to people who stir up laughter in me and who respond to my playfulness. I am fortunate to find such friends among my co-workers, my students, and persons I meet in other settings.

Still, I am particularly grateful for the long and deep impact of these three—Lee, Dave, Donna Beth. Each of them modeled humor and taught and stretched me as to the range, possibilities, and helpfulness of humor. From time to time, each of them comforted me and helped me to get back on track with that humor. Most of all, I laughed with them, enjoyed them, loved them, learned from them, copied them a bit, and grew from them.

My eyes and ears are more open because of their gifts to me. Out of these rich experiences I go on to ask other questions. What kinds of humor are there and which of them fit the work of ministry? What are the functions of humor— what does it contribute to lives and relationships? How does this relate to faith perspective and to the tasks of ministry?

We will next explore the variety of humor strategies that are available to us.

QUESTIONS FOR PERSONAL AND GROUP REFLECTION

1. Who have been your mentors-models in humor, particularly humor as a spiritual practice? Recall at least one and tell another person in your group about that person. What's your richest memory about that person?
2. If you are fortunate enough to have such persons, what are the most important discoveries about humor you take from them?

3. How do you see yourself—as always playful and humorous, sometimes so, seldom so, or never so? If humor / play is part of your life, have you ever completely lost it for a while? If so, what helped the sense of play, joy, and humor come back?
4. Are there persons who would speak of you as their mentor / model of the spiritual practice of humor? If so, what do you recall about times when your humor was helpful to them?
5. What questions about humor do you hope to raise or ideas about humor do you hope to explore before your group has completed this journey?
6. What are you learning about humor as a spiritual practice for you personally?

2

Let Me Count the Ways to Brighten Your Days

(The Varieties of Humor)

Humor is emotional chaos remembered in tranquility.

—James Thurber[1]

For the next two chapters, I want to explore with you unpopular, but important topics. What kinds of humor are there? Does a spiritual practice of humor and play have more possibilities than are often realized? What do these types of humor do, achieve, and accomplish—how do they work? And what effect / impact do they have? What gifts do they give and contributions do they make?

These topics are indeed unpopular, at least with humorists. Long ago, Robert Benchley observed, "Defining and analyzing humor is a pastime of humorless people."[2] Much later, Bob Newhart cautioned, "If I ever see another book called *The Serious Side of Comedy*, I'm going to throw up. I feel like comedy is like that tribe in Africa who doesn't want their pictures taken because they believe a photograph steals part of their soul. The closer you get to understanding humor, the more you begin to lose your sense of humor."[3]

At the same time, we sometimes humor-challenged people may need just what these geniuses of humor decry. For our purposes, it is important to see humor as something that can be investigated, studied,

1. Quoted in *Peter's Quotations*, 498.
2. Ibid.
3. Newhart, *I Shouldn't Even Be Doing This!*, 171.

observed, classified, practiced, increased, and improved. Humor will always still be a surprise, a mystery. Still, with wider awareness we may increase our opportunities and options for play and laughter. It's worth a try!

For the present consider the vastness of humor types.

HOW DOES ONE DO HUMOR?

How many ways are there to make a person laugh? If we want to entertain or be entertained, what are the possibilities?

Evan Esar attempted to answer that—more than a half century ago—in a book titled *The Humor of Humor.* His subtitle promises to explore "The Art and Techniques of Popular Comedy Illustrated by Comic Sayings, Funny Stories and Jocular Traditions through the Centuries." Not only does he list, describe, and give examples of the types of humor in previous and current centuries, he speaks of the "budding science of humor."

This is his attempt to catalogue and classify all the types of humor there are. Space does not permit listing absolutely every type of humor he mentions (some of the distinctions he makes are either quite small or dated), but I will report a large portion of what he notes. Types of humor that Esar mentions include the following:

- The wisecrack (a smart or flippant remark), and the gag (a variety of clever and also flippant replies)—the subjects for these evolve and change with each generation. One example of the gag is the "Knock Knock" joke.
- The epigram (a witty, often paradoxical saying or short poem such as supposed Confucius sayings).
- Riddles and conundrums.
- Jokes.
- Anecdotes.
- Techniques of humor such as the chain (one thing leads to another), the pendulum (back and forth, such as "Good News, Bad News" jokes), blunting, and reversibles (winding up back where you started).
- Humor in speech such as Spoonerisms (mixing up the first letters of words with comic results), "fuddletalk" (humorous imitation

of inebriated talk), tongue twisters, baby talk, dialects, or double talk.

- Word play. While puns come to mind, Esar observes a wide variety of word plays such as the wellerism (a quoted phrase illustrates a concrete instance—a cannibal telling the captured missionary, "we'd love to have you for dinner"); transposer, humor by reversing the order of letters, syllables, words, or sounds ("The more patient pedestrians, the fewer pedestrian patients"); or antonymism, comic effect is produced by using antonyms ("The girl with a future avoids the man with a past").
- Variations on "the fool" such as April Fool jokes, the absent-minded professor, the foolish question. ("'April 1,' quipped Mark Twain, 'is the day upon which we are minded of what we are on the other 364.'")
- Slips and blunders, including malapropisms (the ludicrous misuse of a word), Freudian slips, mistaken identities, typographical errors, and boners—short, pointed mistakes having an amusing effect (A child's test answer: "The equator is a menagerie lion running around the middle of the earth").
- Tricks, for example, practical jokes, or trick bets.
- The twist—taking any form of popular expression and distorting or contorting in some playful way ("No man knows if honesty is the best policy unless he has tried both.").
- Caricatures, of which there are many—the henpecked husband, the efficiency expert, the mad psychiatrist, the hypocritical, otherworldly or super pious clergy, among others.
- Satire—a continuum of types that combine humor and criticism. This includes satire, irony, parody, sarcasm, and burlesque, with nuances of difference among these.
- Funny stories, including shaggy dog stories, tall tales, fables, and more.
- Nonsense, including exaggerations, and (one of my personal favorites) limericks.[4]

4. Esar, *The Humor of Humor.*

One of my limericks:

I'm learned, I'm told, wise and smart.
I know tomes and some poems each by heart.
So I'm humbled to see
'Tis a child and not me
Who can get this computer to start.

And a limerick about the strangeness of the English language:

There was a young girl in the choir
Whose voice rose hoir and hoir.
Till it reached such a height
It was clear out of seight,
And they found it next day in the spoir.

(From Rumors Newsletter, March, 2010)

Is this list exhaustive (even as we acknowledge many variations within each category)? I don't think so. With this impressive collection, Esar has still missed some things or chose to leave them out. His is a list of humor through words.

But there are other types:

- There is also physical action humor (the pie in the face, the pratfall, the Gatorade "bath" for the winning coach).
- Closely related, there is humor using materials (the flower that sprays the onlooker with water, the red rubber nose, trick food, etc.).
- Further, there are sight gags of various types—the unexpected, the shocker, the embarrassing, for example.
- And, combining all of these together, there are playful toys.

These are a few of the omissions that occurred to me after I had gone over it several times.

We might ask another question about this fifty-plus-year-old list. Have the comics since then invented any new kinds of humor? I raise this question in my mind as Mary Ann and I often watch "The Daily Show" and "The Steven Colbert Report." Their humor is fast moving, always on timely issues and themes. They use numerous clips of other shows and events and create visual-physical humor of their own. But, as far as I can tell, the humor they use is much repartee, clever word play, caricature-teasing-heckling, with a good dose of sarcasm and irony. (The bad news is that once you start studying humor, you analyze comedy shows. The good news is that it does not diminish the enjoyment!)

A playful and imaginative mind is a wonderfully entertaining instrument! There are many different ways to make us laugh. Within this list are possibilities for each person to explore, enjoy, and expand.

WHAT ARE DIFFERENT PERSPECTIVES ON HUMOR?

Not only are there many kinds of humor, there are a number of perspectives from which to analyze humor / laughter. In her book, *Comic Laughter*, Marie Collins Swabey discusses ways the various academic disciplines may view this topic.

- When viewed from the biological perspective, some would see laughter as a release of suppressed energy. Others might speak of it as a reversion to infantilism, or, perhaps as an expression of basic organic drives.
- From the sociological perspective, laughter can be considered in two contrasting ways. It may be seen as a means of social control to punish non-conformists. The laughter of ridicule or disdain is much feared. Or, for the non-conformists and persecuted, laughter may be a means to attack and undermine the ruling class or other social structures in turn.
- On the other hand, the psychological perspective may find in merriment an outlet for frustration. Or it may be seen as an acceptable way to express aggression. Sometimes, this humor may be a safe way to talk about the secrets of sexual desire, the fear of death or other unacceptable topics.

Swabey's academic discipline is philosophy, and so she approaches humor-laughter from that perspective. She believes that what is really important

> . . . is that in the laughter of comic insight we achieve a logical moment of truth; . . . We gain an inkling, as it were, of the hang of things, sometimes even a hint of cosmic beneficence. In short, perception of the ludicrous helps us to comprehend both ourselves and the world, making us . . . feel more at home in the universe by aiding in the discernment of values.[5]

That's quite an assertion! From a philosophic point of view, she suggests, laughter may reveal truths about life and the universe that are

5. Swabey, *Comic Laughter*, v.

otherwise hidden from us. We theologians join the philosophers in that expectation, while hoping for even more.

Hold that thought for now. For now, we simply acknowledge that humor can be approached from many points of view, and each tells us something about it that the other perspectives do not.

WHAT DOES HUMOR DO?

Humor can be explored from yet another perspective. Why do people engage humor at all? What goal, what purpose, what function do all these different kinds of humor have in their lives? Peter Berger suggests a basic way of exploring these purposes of humor. In his book, *Redeeming Laughter: The Comic Dimension of Human Experience*, he considers "Comic Forms of Expression." The question is—what are the basic categories of humor and what is the basic purpose of each kind? The answer, in brief, is that the comic can provide diversion, or consolation, or a game of intellect, or a weapon for attack.

On any given day, all four of these types / purposes of humor will be found on the comic pages in the newspaper. Further, in any given year, all four of these types of humor will also be themes in essays, short stories, novels, movies, plays, and TV programs. Let's consider.

The comic as diversion

Laughter is like changing a baby's diaper—it doesn't solve any problems permanently, but it makes things more acceptable for a while.[6]

One type is benign humor, the comic as diversion. This is the simplest, most frequent, most common type of humor. It is the stuff of children's play and their frequent giggles and laughter at little unexpected things. "Benign humor . . . is harmless, even innocent. It is intended to evoke pleasure, relaxation, and good will. It enhances rather than disrupts the flow of everyday life."[7] It is that relaxed moment of amusement that helps one through the day, able to manage all its little irritants. As such, it is a momentary interruption of the more serious activities of living. This type of humor can be enjoyed by oneself as well as with others.

6. Anonymous source, quoted by Sweet, *The Jesus Prescription*, 25.

7. Berger, *Redeeming Laughter*, 99.

One example of this type was that wonderful comedian of the late nineteenth and early twentieth centuries, Will Rogers. Many of his quips were about living sagely. "Never slap a man who's chewing tobacco . . . Never kick a cow chip on a hot day . . . Never miss a good chance to shut up . . . Always drink upstream from the herd . . . Good judgment comes from experience, and a lot of that comes from bad judgment . . . Lettin' the cat outta the bag is a whole lot easer'n puttin' it back."[8] There were also his comments on congress and government preceded by his well known statement, "All I know is what I read in the papers." While there was a great amount of kidding about government leaders, there was no serious attack. He once commented, "I don't think I ever hurt any man's feelings by my little gags. I know I never willfully did it. When I have to do that to make a living I will quit."[9] Rogers' most famous quote, "I never met a man I didn't like" is all the more significant when the context and full quote is known. He was on a visit to the Soviet Union and wanted to meet Communist leader Leon Trotsky, but was prevented from doing so. He regretted this and stated, "I bet you if I had met him and had a chat with him, I would have found him a very interesting and human fellow, for I have never yet met a man I didn't like."[10]

This type of humor doesn't stop with Will Rogers. There are numerous places where this benign, diversion-providing humor is found. A number of the types of humor that Esar mentioned are widely used in this way, for example, Knock Knock jokes, puns and other plays on words, humorous quotations, and limericks. On the comics page in the newspaper, Peanuts, Family Tree, Marmaduke, Garfield, and Dennis the Menace are examples of this type. Some of Mark Twain's humor was in this mode, although he also ventured into other types. Contemporary humorists such as Garrison Keillor often operate largely in this way.

We must note that not all benign humor is G-rated. The subjects explored may range over many topics. Not all are necessarily fit for the ears of the young.

This type of humor poses no threat to all the realities of ordinary life. "They provide a vacation from the latter's worries, a harmless diversion from which one can return, refreshed to the business of living. Yet there is a kind of magic here too . . . This enchantment has its own value,

8. These quotes were in a circulated email I received on 11/17/06.

9. Berger, *Redeeming Laughter*, 107.

10. Quoted in note 12 on 115 of Berger, *Redeeming Laughter*.

perhaps even its own moral status."[11] One thing the comic can be, then, is the one who relaxes, refreshes, renews those who recognize, enjoy, and enter in to this kind of humor.

The comic as consolation

Lost—Dog, faded brown, three legs, one ear missing,
blind left eye, broken tail, recently neutered.
Answers to name, 'Lucky.' Sorry, no rewards.

— Newspaper ad

Another type is tragicomedy—the comic as consolation. This form may be described as laughter through tears. "Tragicomedy . . . is mellow, forgiving. It does not bring about a profound catharsis, but it is moving nonetheless. Above all else, it consoles. This consolation may or may not have religious overtones . . . [T]he tragic is not banished, not defied, not absorbed. It is, as it were, momentarily suspended."[12]

Tragicomedy operates closer to the pain of human experience than benign humor does. However, it is not "black humor" such as gallows humor, for example, that defies the tragic. Nor is it grotesque humor that absorbs tragedy into an absurd universe.

Rather, this is the attitude that claims the goodness and power of life and living in the face of all that would deny or destroy that. It does not wipe out the tragedies of life, but it helps to make them bearable.

Humor of consolation has its limits. Sometimes tragedy is so great and so deep, that, in all probability, no humor should be attempted. Still it may be appropriate gently to inquire—is there any room for remembrances that bring smiles to our faces?

The American humorist Charlie Chaplin was a master of tragicomedy. As he went through his struggles with machines, troubles with people who ignored or abused him, he always bore those injuries in ways that made us smile and chuckle. Chaplin once said, "Playful pain—that's what humor is. The minute a thing is over-tragic, it is funny."[13]

11. Ibid., 114.
12. Ibid., 117.
13. Quoted in Mullen, *Laughing Out Loud*, 113.

The late comedian Roger Dangerfield and his frequent complaint "I don't get no respect" is yet another example. On the comics pages, "For Better or Worse" with all the travails of a three generation family (aging, grieving, breaking up, weddings), "Ziggy" a modern day Charlie Chaplin, and "Zits" poking fun at the generation gap provide tragicomic humor daily.

Berger's main example was the Yiddish writer, Sholem Aleichem who lived in the late nineteenth and early twentieth centuries. From time to time, he lived in a Ukrainian Shtetl, a small Jewish village. This was during a time of terrible conditions when Jews were restricted as to where they could live, what they could do for an occupation and were classified as inferior subjects. Physical attacks on their persons and property were not uncommon.

In such a setting, Aleichem's writing is full of comic characters and situations. He saw that his mission was to give voice to what he called an "orphan people" and to create laughter in a wretched world. One of his most famous stories was about Tevya the milkman. And, as you may have anticipated, his stories formed the basis for the acclaimed musical, *Fiddler on the Roof.*

Others add their witness to this as a powerful and helpful type of humor. Frederick Buechner notes, "Laughter comes from as deep a place as tears come from, and in a way, it comes from the same place."[14] Viktor Frankl, holocaust survivor and creator of logotherapy (therapy through meaning and purpose in life) commented on those days of suffering in the death camps, "Humor was another of the soul's weapons in the fight for self-preservation. It is well known that humor, more than anything else in the human makeup, can afford an aloofness and an ability to rise above any situation, even if only for a few seconds."[15]

We will certainly revisit this type of humor. It needs to be a significant part of any caregiver's repertoire (and an important resource for oneself), along with wisdom when and when not to use it, offered with sensitivity to the hurting persons with whom we offer care.

14. Ibid., 9.

15. Frankl, *Man's Search for Meaning*, 63–64.

The comic as game of intellect

Still another type of humor is wit, engaging humor as an intellectual game. In wit the comic uses humor to gain insight and express reality that might be otherwise missed. It is the use of intelligence and thought functions in humor. Granted that all humor uses intellect, in this form the intellect is more prominent and may be the only purpose of the exercise.

The use of intelligent wit may disclose incongruence that is not perceived in a serious attitude. The laughter may be an opening for truth, but there are times when the truth is deceptive.

Wit may engage intellect and language but also behavior. Berger adds, "Wit in this form has no interest beyond itself, is dispassionate, detached from any practical agenda." Wit becomes a comic's "toy." "Wit always employs paradox and irony . . . The most effective wit employs spare means to achieve a rich result. Wit is sharp, pithy, pointed."[16]

In western culture, the joke is one of the most common forms of wit. "Jokes can be described as very short stories that end with a comically startling statement."[17] This is the "punch line" which indicates the intent to deliver some sort of insight.

Another wide spread form of this humor is the epigram. This is a compact statement or definition that delivers a pronouncement on some subject in an entertaining way.

H. L. Mencken was one of the masters of epigrams. Here are a couple of his well known ones:

> HUMOR FOR LEXOPHILES
> (Lovers of Words)
>
> I wondered why the baseball was getting bigger. Then it hit me.
>
> Police were called to a day care, where a three-year-old was resisting a rest.
>
> The roundest knight at King Arthur's round table was Sir Cumference.
>
> To write with a broken pencil is pointless.
>
> When fish are in schools, they sometimes take debate.
>
> The short fortune teller who escaped from prison was a small medium at large.
>
> When the smog lifts in Los Angeles, U.C.L.A. (from an email)

16. Berger, *Redeeming Laughter*, 136.
17. Ibid.

"*Conscience* is the inner voice which warns us that someone may be looking."

"*Puritanism*—The haunting fear that someone somewhere may be happy."[18]

The caution is that many jokes and epigrams that may be funny are not necessarily true,—or, I might add, accurate, fair, sensitive, or up-building. While both the Mencken epigrams above may be worth a chuckle, they are both inaccurate and very limited in scope. Conscience may be much nobler than he describes. His quip on Puritans is one-sided, and highly misleading, but has been unthinkingly accepted by many as an accurate description.

If that is a humorless response to Mencken's wit, so be it. (At least he roused me to thought!) While humor can reveal truths otherwise hidden, an important caution is that it can also blind or mislead people. That is the risk and the dilemma of those of us who engage humor as a spiritual practice of ministry.

The comic as weapon

There is another type of humor, satire, "the deliberate use of the comic for purposes of attack."[19] The attack may be against institutions and their representatives. Both governmental and religious institutions are often the subject of satire. Or it may be directed against individuals, professions, theories, or literary modes.

As we noted, wit may also include this element of critique and attack. In satire, the aggressive intent becomes the central motif, the reason for doing an exercise in humor. "Its emotional tone is typically malicious, even if the motive for the attack is this or that high principle . . . Benevolent satire is an oxymoron."[20]

Satire may proceed from two levels of influence and power. Persons may engage in this type of humorous criticism as approximate equals, and this is often done in political contests.

Or sometimes, this is one of the last resort methods of the underling, the defeated, and the mistreated. Persons may not have the political, police, or military power to deal with those who oppress them. However,

18. Ibid., quoted on 139.

19. Ibid., 157.

20. Ibid.

they still have the freedom of their thoughts, their ideas, and their humor. This can be exercised to keep alive the fire of resistance. It can also make others sharply aware of the little minds of those who rule and of the injustices they administer.

Satirists who operate from a more privileged position still may see trends, ideas, and movements they view as wrong and dangerous. Satire always includes fantasy (sometimes grotesque), a standpoint based on moral norms, and an object of attack. They engage this medium to destroy, question, or cut down to size the perceived threat.

Examples of satire might include Doonesbury in the comic strips and the cartoons on the editorial page. The satirical novel is a frequent form and includes, among many others, George Orwell's *Animal Farm* and Tom Wolfe's *Bonfire of the Vanities.* Political columnists such as the late Art Buchwald and the late Molly Ivans illustrate another possible avenue. TV personalities such as Rush Limbaugh and Al Franken (before he exchanged the broadcast booth for the Senate chamber) engage it freely. Certainly, politicians use this humor as attack on each other. And it is not unknown among religious people attacking both individuals and points of view with which they take issue.

Berger concludes, "Satire too is, so to speak, epistemologically-neutral. Its rhetorical power does not mean necessarily that its portrayal of reality is accurate. Satire, like wit can distort reality, even lie."[21] (We will later explore some contrasts between satire and irony.)

Further, satire and its practice of debunking can become an ingrained habit. Persons attracted to it can fall into this approach when it is appropriate, but also when it is not. It can be overdone, a one note approach to every issue, topic, or opponent.

Still, with these temptations and dangers admitted, satire may be a valuable gift if humor is to be a vehicle of revelation as we suggested at the beginning of this chapter.

AND SO—

Our survey of perspectives on, types of, and reasons for humor stirs both possibility and question. What does all this have to do with spiritual practices? How does this information relate to the life of ministry and church? Are there types that should be included and some that should

21. Ibid., 172.

be excluded in a spiritually rich life? What enrichment of ministry and cautions for leadership and care giving need to be observed? We will continue to explore those questions, but first, there is another aspect to consider— what specifically does humor do? What happens when humor is employed? What are its gifts? It is to this topic that we will next turn.

QUESTIONS FOR PERSONAL AND GROUP REFLECTION

1. If you read comics, which comic strip do you read first? What do you particularly like about it?
2. Of all the types of humor mentioned in this chapter, which do you enjoy most when others use it? Which do you most like to use yourself?
3. Which of the possible uses of humor seem most fitting for church leaders and ministers? Which, if any, should be avoided at all costs, in your opinion?
4. What did this chapter miss—whether of kinds of humor or uses of humor? What would you add?
5. From this smorgasbord of humor possibilities which do you comfortably embrace in a spiritual practice of humor and play? Which do you accept but with reservations? Which do you reject?
6. What discoveries / insights about humor as a spiritual practice do you take from our conversation so far? What unanswered questions has it stirred in you?

3

"There's a Heck of a Lot of Medicine in Fun"

(*The Contributions of Humor*)

It is the uncensored sense of humor . . .
which is the ultimate therapy for man in society.

—EVAN ESAR[1]

AFTER BEING REMINDED, AND possibly stretched a little about the vast range of types of humor, we have another question. What does humor do—what does it accomplish? As to our contention that the practice of humor helps caring persons heal and have greater staying power, how does it do that? Why do people engage in this strange thing called humor?

Are those dumb questions—obviously, people do humor for fun, enjoyment, relaxation—or is there more? What will the addition of humor to any situation contribute to individuals? To the relationships between them?

The answer to these questions appears to be "much indeed." A number of authors and a variety of studies report many good things that humor can bring forth. I will report and reflect on these in a moment.

However, I must tell you there is some disagreement about what is actually known on this topic, particularly in regard to physical health benefits. On the positive side, there is "anecdotal evidence"—stories and experiences as well as studies on the power of humor in many areas of life. A new aspect of this is "laughing yoga." In 1995, Dr. Madan Kataria

1. Quoted in *Peter's Quotations*, 497.

launched the first Laughter Club in Mumbai, India, and there are now at least 6,000 Social Laughter Clubs (regularly engaging laughing yoga—laughter without jokes or humor) in 60 countries. These participants offer countless testimonials (and some supporting studies) to the power of daily laughter on their health and their sense of wellbeing.[2]

On the negative side, there is awareness just how difficult it is to investigate human subjects and their emotions. There is vagueness about what exactly we are studying—is it a sense of humor, or laughter (which can be without humor and which also can be forced or spontaneous), or a broad positive playful attitude, or a hospitable atmosphere for such things? (For my purposes, the precision really doesn't matter. I hope for as many of those—humor, laughter, play, atmosphere—as possible. Admittedly, it does make precise scientific studies difficult.)

Also, a scientific study needs large enough samples to be statistically significant and there need to be "control" groups—persons that do not have the humor component who can be compared with those who do. Such studies, so far, are infrequent, and indeed some of the results seem to contradict earlier studies, calling some of the most optimistic conclusions into question.

A further question is about the actual impact of humor / laughter. Does it contribute to the cure, or is it mostly an analgesic (reducing the pain but not curing), or is it a placebo—an inert substance that people *think* has healing qualities and therefore claim them?[3]

I will take an optimistic—but not over-optimistic—stance on this topic. This means sharing what my experience and life says is true, aware that that more research may modify some of these claims. To be sure, I cannot absolutely prove much of this. Consider the various benefits I suggest and then reflect upon your life and experiences and evaluate what I say to see if you believe it is true.

PHYSICAL BENEFITS

"If we took what we know about the medical benefits of laughter and bottled it up, it would require FDA approval," says Lee Berk, a professor at the University of California at Irvine.[4] Dr. Berk is among those who are convinced about both physical and psychological benefits of humor.

2. Laughter Yoga International, "Laughter Yoga As Laughter Therapy."

3. See Provine, *Laughter, A Scientific Investigation*, 189–207 and Capps, *Laughter Ever After*, 1–21.

4. Quoted in Amen, *Making a Good Brain Great*, 175.

He joins a long list of those who testify thus. Centuries ago, the writer of Proverbs wrote, "A cheerful heart is a good medicine, but a downcast spirit dries up the bones." (17:22). The great American humorist, Mark Twain, in his book, *Tom Sawyer*, wrote, "The old man laughed joyously and loud, shook up the details of his anatomy from head to foot, saying that such a laugh was money in a man's pocket because it cut down on doctor's bills like everything."[5] Or as another American humorist, Josh Billings put it, "There ain't much fun in medicine, but there's a heck of a lot of medicine in fun."

> In Seattle the Wizz-Kids, a softball team made up of kidney and liver transplant recipients, beat the Heartbeats, a team of heart transplant recipients, in a game that turned on several close calls by the umpires, all cornea transplant recipients.
>
> ("Sickie Awards" *Health*, January-February, 1993, 53, quoted in Sweet, *The Jesus Prescription for a Healthy Life*, 178.)

The Jewish mime Samuel Avital suggests that laughter exercises every cell in the body, "When you laugh, the whole system vibrates, a dancing diaphragm, dancing cells. All the cells are happy, and when you are happy you have a longer life. If you don't furnish your cells with this vibration of dancing which we intellectually call 'laughing,' you are robbing them of life. So laughter is a transformer."[6]

Laughter is not only exercise—it is *aerobic* exercise. "Dr. William Fry, Stanford University, claims one minute of laughter is equal to ten minutes on the rowing machine." More oxygen is taken in during laughter, which contributes to a sense of well-being. Further, this is aerobic exercise suitable for all, including those confined to wheelchair or bed.[7]

This understanding moved from folk wisdom to scientific respectability with the now more than thirty-year-old written experience of Norman Cousins. In an essay in the *New England Journal of Medicine* and later in a book, *Anatomy of an Illness*, Cousins told of being seriously ill with ankylosing spondylitis. This is a chronic inflammatory rheumatic

5. Twain, *The Adventures of Tom Sawyer*, 90.

6. Quoted in Sweet, *The Jesus Prescription*, 28.

7. "10 Good Reasons to Laugh for No Reason", a handout from Plaza Wellspring, www.plazawellspring.com.

disease of the lower back that results in prodigious pain. When treatments were not helping and his prognosis was grim, he checked out of the hospital and into a hotel room. There he engaged—with his doctor's cooperation—in a self treatment plan that included hours of laughter while watching Marx Brothers and Candid Camera films.

He discovered that ten minutes of laughter provided him with two hours of pain-free sleep. Further, his sedimentation rates slowly but progressively improved. In time, he experienced full recovery from an illness that was threatening his life.[8]

Cousins and others expanded their view that not only humor / laughter but the whole range of positive human emotions contribute both to pain reduction and to healing. This broader definition of humor is also my perspective when I speak of the contributions of humor. Humor, in this view, does indeed include play and playfulness, optimism and hopefulness, thoughts, feelings, behaviors; all this and more contribute to a person's physical well being.

Here are some of the specific ways some studies indicate that humor-laughter-positive emotions may well benefit us physically:

- Lower blood pressure. (One experiment discovered that a ten minute laughter session lead to a reduction of 10–20 mm in blood pressure. Of course, this does not mean humorous / laughing people should cancel their medications.)
- Trigger endorphins, brain chemicals that can bring on euphoria and decrease pain.
- Enhance our immune system—"Gamma-interferon, a disease-fighting protein, rises with laughter. So do B-cells which produce disease destroying antibodies, and T-cells which orchestrate the body's immune response."[9]
- Reduce unhelpful hormones. "Laughter lowers the flow of dangerous stress hormones that suppress the immune system, raise blood pressure, and increase the number of platelets, which cause clots and potentially fatal coronary artery blockages."[10]

8. Cousins, *Anatomy of an Illness*.

9. Amen, *Making a Good Brain Great*, 175.

10. Ibid.

- Relax and improve one's muscle tone, respiratory functioning and cardiovascular system. "For cardiovascular and respiratory functions, the effect of laughter is especially significant. When we laugh, our rhythmic breathing becomes spasmodic and heart rate, blood pressure, and muscular tension increase. When laughter subsides, however, these functions often drop temporarily below normal and result in feelings of relaxation which may last as long as forty-five minutes after the last laugh."[11] Laughter also tones facial muscles and expressions. It has been noted that people even look younger while laughing!

These findings square with my experience. I know when I am ill, I am drawn to humorous story (during my last hospitalization, I read the latest Garrison Keiller novel, watched TV sporting events, and enjoyed visits from playful friends. All of this, I believe, contributed to my recovery.)

Scientific knowledge about the physical gifts of humor and other positive emotions will grow and quite possibly change. Still, what is known point to what a great ally these attitudes and emotions are, both in healthy living and when contending with illness. No one would say that this is enough in itself. If laughter / humor is good medicine, it should be taken with all other possible steps for good medical treatment and holistic health care. I do say it is a valuable resource for my self-care and ministry and for yours.

PSYCHOLOGICAL-EMOTIONAL-RELATIONAL BENEFITS

When I'm happy I feel like crying, but when I'm sad
I don't feel like laughing. I think it's better to be happy.
That way you get two feelings for the price of one.

—Lily Tomlin as Edith Ann[12]

The benefits go beyond the physical ones. Humor enhances our inner life and the way we view the world as well as our relationships with other people. Humor may calm and relax us, stir thoughts of other possibilities, or lift us out of a blue mood. True, humor does not cure deep depression

11. Donnelly, "Divine Folly," 395.
12. quoted by Klein, *The Healing Power of Humor*, xvii.

or extreme grief, nor should we expect it to. (In chapter 6 we will explore when, if ever, to introduce humor with depressed or grieving people.) But much of our humor contributes to a sense of well-being.

Nuances of this psychological benefit are explored by Donald Capps in his fascinating book, *A Time to Laugh: The Religion of Humor*. He goes beyond the generalities of the preceding paragraph and suggests five more specific psychological benefits of humor. The medium of humor for Capps in this book is primarily the joke, which may influence some of what he says. We will consider his points below but feel free to range more widely, as we explore these gifts.

Humor may save psychic resources

Humor helps us cope.

One of the first to note this was Sigmund Freud in his essays on humor. He pointed out that while we humans tend to live beyond our psychic means, humor is—so to speak—an "economical" way to deal with some of these stressors. At one point Freud speaks of three forms of psychic resource drain: painful emotions, costly inhibitions, and difficult thinking.

Jokes and other forms of humor or laughter reduce and circumvent the pain these stressors would otherwise cause. Through a humorous approach, one may experience some sense of triumph in the midst of what would otherwise be dire circumstances.

For example, Freud told many Jewish beggar jokes at a time when his career was being severely hampered due to prejudice against him and his Jewishness. Still another example is the widespread use of humor to deal with death anxiety. The anxiety may be about dying itself, funerals, judgment, or life after death. In each aspect, there is no lack of jokes and other humor.

There are jokes aplenty about costly inhibitions as well. Limericks and other satirical pieces abound about clergy who advocate sexual purity or financial sacrifice but cannot keep their own counsel. Some ethnic humor may playfully assume laxity of sexual morals in one targeted group—and give voice to one's own sexual anxieties.

Painful emotions, great fears, and costly inhibitions are often found together and closely related. Lest they overwhelm, humor is apt to spring up to name these "dragons and then cut them down to size, to something we can live with."[13]

13. Capps, *A Time to Laugh*, 7–40. Capps reflects on several of Freud's writings, notably *Jokes and Their Relation to the Unconscious*.

Humor may serve as a stimulus to self-identity creation or recognition

Perhaps, humor will help us know ourselves better. Capps leads us in this further discovery by exploring Norman N. Holland's psychology of humor. Holland begins his book with a line from a Denise Levertov poem, "She continued to laugh on some days, to cry on others, unfolding the design of her identity."[14]

Holland suggests that rather than considering what humor is in general, a more important approach is what humor is for a particular individual. Why does he, or she, or I, someone in particular laugh? To investigate this, Holland designed an experiment in which students were asked to look at several cartoons, say which ones they considered funny and why. Capps did a similar experiment with a number of jokes, from which persons could select what touched their funny bone and tell why.

> "We think about our feelings and get migraine headaches; We swallow our feelings and get ulcers; We carry the weight of our feelings and get back pain; We sit on our feelings and get hemorrhoids."
>
> —James Zullo, (quoted in Sweet, *The Jesus Prescription for a Healthy Life*, 101)

The thesis behind these studies is that we are what we laugh at. Or perhaps, more accurately, what we laugh at tells us a good bit about ourselves. For example, small children love stories about animals and birds. This may well be an expression of the child's natural curiosity. Further, the stories may deal with issues about which the children are anxious.

At the same time, animal and bird jokes may be useful for adults in exploring their identity themes. What kind of animal jokes do we like? With what animals do we identify? To what dilemmas—or for that matter, what cleverness, characteristics, courage—of the chosen animal do we connect?

Pause and reflect for a moment. Think about the jokes or other humor you have enjoyed—from others or from you—in the last two weeks. Jot them down. Then ask yourself, "What does this list tell me about me?" (As I do this exercise myself, I see a preponderance of jokes about

14. Capps, *A Time to Laugh*, 41, quoting Holland, *Laughing: A Psychology of Humor*, 9.

aging. I know why—I had a recent birthday and am probably giving voice both to my fears and my hopes about my own growing older.)

Humor is great fun. With thought and self-reflection, it may also tell us a great deal about ourselves.

Humor may express intimacy or contribute to that intimacy

Victor Borge once said, "Humor is the shortest distance between two people." Indeed, that is another of its great gifts. People come together in a group for the first time, feeling strange, uncertain, and tense. Someone tells a joke, laughter breaks the tension, and folks begin to relax into being a group with good vibes. Or, later in the group's life, disagreements and arguments may arise. Again, humor may break the tension, disarm defensiveness, help one see the other side, or at least help one recognize and care for the person on the other side.

Capps explores this gift by considering the telling of jokes as a communal act. There is a teller and at least one hearer. One of the satisfactions in successful joke transactions is the sense that teller and hearer(s) are joined in feeling. Ted Cohen comments, "There is a recurring pattern in successful joke transactions: many jokes presuppose beliefs, knowledge, and/or feelings shared by the teller and the listener, and when the listener activates these, thereby completing the design of the joke, a sense of intimacy is achieved."[15]

This sense of community may come in "problem-solving jokes," as an unexpected solution stirs mutual enjoyment. For example, consider the popularity of the "How do you change a light bulb?" jokes. Further, intimacy may arise out of persons of an ethnic group sharing "in-jokes" about themselves—or religious groups doing so, for that matter. Intimacy may even be a part of friendly competitive joking between ethnic or religious groups.

Community-building humor may have as its topic the search for intimacy. This may include such topics as a guy goes into a bar jokes, Jewish mother jokes, marriage conflict and resolution jokes. There is intimacy in laughing at infirmities such as the perils of aging, the decline of sexual prowess, the limitations of the world of medicine or psychiatrists, or counselors, or clergy.

15. Capps, *A Time to Laugh*, 69. He is quoting Cohen, *Jokes: Philosophical Thoughts on Joking Matters*, 25.

There is often a stretching of boundaries or propriety in this kind of humor, a testing that can backfire on the one attempting it. And so the community building gift of humor is by no means automatic or indiscriminate. Timing, sensitivity, moral considerations of what, when, and where to use it are important.

Nonetheless, the possibility of creation, or increase, or restoration of intimacy is a frequent gift of humor. So many awkward, ambiguous, or tense gatherings have been put at ease by laughing together. It has served as invitation to the friendship and community that can emerge.

And, as I related in chapter one, humor can be the cement that binds soul friends together over the years and over the decades.

Humor may aid the "gentle art of re-framing"

Reframing is developing the ability to see the same issues / problems from more than one perspective. If, for example, a person thinks there is only one way to deal with a dilemma and discovers there are two or more ways to deal with that problem, s/he has reframed it. There are many ways to reframe an issue. Each can be helpful in the human struggle for wholeness.

Humor is a vital tool in this growth process in a number of ways. It might allow the relationship between caregiver and care receiver to become more relaxed and intimate. Laughing together can increase trust and receptivity, which might in turn facilitate communication.

A humorous way of expressing the dilemma may increase this understanding and communication. Humor may help a person see that a problem is smaller or less personally threatening than previously imagined. In chapter one, I described how my friend Lee helped me reframe church conflict and criticism issues by restating them as Bob Newhart routines.

Or, humor may invite the courage to face "ghosts"—huge, frightening issues which are ignored or denied (or, to change the image, the unacknowledged "elephant in the room" so to speak). There may be terminal illness, or addiction, or abuse, or divorce, or other present and unspoken topics that need to be named and discussed. Humor may ask or give permission to start talking about the taboo subject. Thus the reframing is around a picture that is more accurate and truthful than the one with "ghosts" and other hidden realities.

Humor can stir imagination and creativity

Humor might stimulate imagination and creativity in so many areas of life. Think of a time when a group is brainstorming and someone comes up with an outlandish suggestion. Do not ideas, suggestions, spontaneity, and freedom flow more freely after that? One "off-the-wall" suggestion stirs groans and chuckles, but at the same time it stimulates even zanier suggestions. People laugh and relax into their joint creativity, and things begin to happen.

Humor can see things from a different perspective, can imagine another way. Thus it is a close partner to much creativity.

These, then, are at least some of the psychological-emotional-relational gifts of humor. But there is more. Humor can be enriching to religious intuitions and to one's spiritual life as well.

RELIGIOUS / SPIRITUAL BENEFITS

Humor is a strong part of the "tie that binds"

The word "religion" comes from the Latin word "ligare" which means to bind or bind together. The root for the word religion, then, is the same as for the word ligament which is defined as "a bond or tie connecting one thing with another," and "a band of tough tissue connecting bones or holding organs in place." Seen this way, religion is that which binds people to one another and to God. This is classically expressed in the well-loved hymn "Blest be the tie that binds our hearts in Christian love."

In turn, we can see humor as part of the "tough tissue" that binds Christians together in love. We in religious organizations need humor. It is essential for our life with each other and with our Creator.

This is even truer, or perhaps especially true, when the humor is about religion itself. Capps comments, "While jokes about religion frequently make light work of religion, challenging its pretensions and flights of grandiosity, this does not mean that they are not in the service of religion."[16] We have been saying that self-humor is usually a healthy type. Self-humor about our faith, our church, our denomination—particularly if arises out of love and perhaps a "lover's quarrel"—may be good both for our churches and for ourselves.

16. Capps, *A Time to Laugh*, 169.

Humor may be a part of "soul maintenance"

Humor helps us accept our earthy, human, sometimes down-side. To appreciate this contribution of humor, consider the differences between the concepts of spirit, self, and soul. Spirit is that aspect which aspires to greater heights; it is something ineffable and inexpressible.

Capps concentrates on soul. A possible definition of soul is "vital or essential part, quality, etc." Soul may well be associated with the night, the moon (lunacy) and death. If the self may emanate from the brain and the spirit from the heart, the bodily location of the soul may be the liver. What the soul contributes are powers of regeneration, particularly from "returning to its central concerns, its formative influences, its grounding in time and place."[17]

In this connection, consider ethnic jokes that concentrate on the stupidity of the named group. These jokes are not so much about the identified group as about the teller. Such jokes enable the tellers to express their personal and collective anxieties about failure.

The theory is that as the teller disassociates oneself from the failure/stupidity in the joke, the person is also expressing the tension between the spirit and the soul. If the spirit is the aspect of self that aspires to greater heights, soul on the other hand, is that part that keeps us rooted.

Jokes about such stupidity or bumbling or misunderstanding or failure may be seen as the soul's attempt to comfort the spirit. They imply it is all right to fail and to fall. For wherever you land, you cannot fall out of this world, and wherever you land is not a bad place to be.

Margaret Baim and Loretta LaRoche identify this gift more directly by suggesting three things humor makes possible: (1) humor gives one a break from the ongoing stress and "buys time" for being creative in altering one's otherwise automatic responses to the stress; (2) humor restores or replenishes depleted emotional and spiritual resources; (3) humor has an upholding / sustaining quality that helps one persist in coping with hard realities, whether these are personal failure or hard blows form others. In this connection, they quote the nineteenth-century American clergyman, Henry Ward Beecher, "A person without a sense of humor is like a wagon without springs—jolted by every pebble in the road."[18]

17. Ibid., 11.

18. Baim and LaRoche, "Jest 'n Joy," 270.

My wife Mary Ann laughed when she saw a refrigerator magnet at a store, and so I bought it for her. It said, "Hang on to your husband. He might come back into fashion." I laughed, too, even though it is about me! Its sub-text is that while long term marriage has disappointments, changes, and adjustments, we keep on, forgiving—and smiling. And humor helps.

As we negotiate the delicate balance between all the aspirations of our upper call and our all too persistent frail humanity (our soul), humor intervenes. Its message: "I can live with this, I can cope, and I can manage. And, as to the more lofty realms, I'll keep trying."

And, as we learn to forgive ourselves, our tough outer edges soften. And thus, we learn to forgive the other. We may even discover something to laugh about in the real or supposed offense.

Cal Samra cites this "Clown's Prayer"

Lord, as I stumble through this life, help me create more laughter than tears, dispense more happiness than gloom, spread more cheer than despair.

Never let me grow so big that I will fail to see the wonder in the eyes of a child, or the twinkle in the eyes of the aged.

Never let me forget that I am a clown, that my work is to cheer people up, make them happy, and make them laugh, make them forget momentarily all the unpleasant things in their lives.

Never let me acquire the financial success to the point where I will discontinue calling upon my Creator in the hour of need, or acknowledging and thanking him in the hour of plenty.

And in my final moment, may I hear you whisper: "When you made MY people smile, you made ME smile."

(*The Joyful Noiseletter*).

Humor invites healing and holiness

Humor is a pre-condition to our healing and our growing in holiness. The self-awareness of which we just spoke helps us "to get out of the way, to loosen our grip, to lessen our need to control, and to let God be God."[19] A sense of humor helps us in this because it encourages us not

19. Donnelly, "Divine Folly," 392–93.

to take ourselves too seriously, for when we do, it is almost impossible to grow in holiness.

Significant things happen in our healing and spiritual growth when we face the truth about ourselves. Note how similar the words "humor" and "humility" are. (Other words sharing the same root include "human" and "humus.") A true sense of humor, just like a true sense of humility requires searching honesty about oneself,—no disguise and no pretense. Most of us are very good at avoiding such honesty. That's why humor may slip by our mental and spiritual blocks. Then it opens our hearts and minds to the grace that is already awaiting us and the growth in the spirit to which we are invited.

Humor brings back perspective and keeps things there. It punctures pretensions and invites humility. Conrad Hyers was right on target when he noted, "Humor apart from holiness may be irresponsible; but holiness apart from humor is inhuman . . . Faith without humor becomes fanaticism. Humor without faith becomes cynicism."[20]

St. Teresa of Avila once prayed, "From somber, sullen, serious saints, deliver us Lord." Amen to that. Thanks be to God for all God's gifts, including the gifts of humor and laughter.

QUESTIONS FOR PERSONAL AND GROUP REFLECTION

1. What, if any, physical health benefits have you experienced from humor?
2. When, if ever, has humor been helpful to you in living with pain or with a problem?
3. When, if ever, has humor been a helpful tool when caring for other hurting people?
4. When has humor been a part of helping you draw close to one other person or to a group? When, if ever, has humor been a factor in building up tension between you and others?
5. When has humor helped you "reframe" an issue or a problem?
6. When has humor been part of the tough tissue that helped a church or other religious group hold together?

20. Hyers, *Holy Laughter*, 208.

7. When has humor been stimulus to, or part of, your spiritual growth?
8. What has this chapter missed? What other benefits and gifts does humor have for you?
9. What are you discovering about the spiritual practice of humor?

4

Why Did Sarah Laugh?

(An Exploration of Humor in the Bible)

The total absence of humour from the Bible
is one of the most singular things in all literatures.

—A. N. WHITEHEAD[1]

The Hebrew Scriptures are filled with a sense of playfulness, especially with the language . . . Satire, gentle wit, and even farce abound in almost every book . . . The Hebrew Bible sings. It laughs. It makes bad jokes and shows a tendency for slapstick.

–EUGENE FISHER[2]

READ AND COMPARE THE two statements given above. With which do you agree? On this topic—humor in the Bible—do you expect to see a series of blank pages or an extremely short chapter?

What we discover about humor in the Bible matters a great deal in our conversation. As we consider a spiritual practice of humor and play, we need to make a determination. Is such a search grounded in and compatible with our sacred scriptures? Or, is it a new, rootless suggestion? When you turn to the Holy Bible do you expect to find smiles, chuckles and guffaws?

1. Quoted by Whedbee, *The Bible and the Comic*, 1.
2. Fisher, "The Divine Comedy," 571–72.

There are those who say, "No, absolutely not." For example, Charles Baudelaire once noted that in general, "Holy books never laugh, to whatever nations they belong."

WHY DON'T WE SEE BIBLICAL HUMOR AND LAUGH?

On the other hand, Bible scholars have demonstrated that such statements reveal a profound misunderstanding of some aspects of scripture. But first, we must ask if indeed there is humor in scripture, why has it been missed so often? There are a number of reasons.

Most basically, we fail to see the humor in scripture because we do not expect to see it there. If we read to find God and God's will revealed, we may have our reverent antennae up and our humor antennae down. A Chinese proverb suggests that ninety percent of what we see comes from behind our eyes. Somehow we have not expected a holy book to be a humorous book, and we have found what we expected and have not found what we did not expect.

Further, over-familiarity may dull our awareness of the humor in scriptures. We have read certain texts and heard them explained from other perspectives. The surprise humor has been dimmed.

By contrast, Elton Trueblood told of seriously reading from Matthew for family devotions when his four-year-old son burst out laughing. Elton had just read "Why do you see the speck in your neighbor's eye but do not notice the log in your own eye?" (Matt 7:3) With fresh and playful ears, the little boy laughed out loud at the comic impossibility in the statement. This was an "aha" moment for Trueblood. He began looking for the humor in Jesus' life and teaching and found it many places that he had missed before. He later wrote of his discoveries in the book, *The Humor of Christ*.[3]

Moreover, much of biblical humor involves intricate word play—puns, riddles, plays on names of geographical places or persons, and witty rejoinders. This needs a developed knowledge of the biblical languages. Indeed, humor is one of the last things a person learns when attempting to master a new language; it comes only with a comfort, an extensive vocabulary, and skill to discern nuances. Further, wordplay humor loses something in translation and often does not translate well at all. Skilled biblical linguistic scholars and commentators will need to unearth much of these aspects of humor for us.

3. Trueblood, *The Humor of Christ*, 9.

With all of this, some may agree with an early reader / reviewer of this chapter who commented, "It's interesting, but it's not funny." This is understandable. While some humor is universal, there are cultural styles and conventions of humor. Even in the present day, the differences in humor between British and Americans, men and women, or Texans and New Englanders may help us understand our difficulty of grasping all that was humorous in an ancient, near eastern culture. There are forms, styles, expectations of that culture that will need to be understood. Only then will we hear the humorous impact that some of these Bible accounts had on the first hearers. And, given the vast distance in cultures, what must have been raucous humor then may stir only a small smile—if that—from us.

True, there may be a "you had to be there" quality to some of this humor. I believe that the awareness that humor is there at all, with all of this glorious variety, is of great import. And I, for one, delight at the mischievousness, playfulness, and creativity of these fellow comics, thousands of years and miles away. See what you think.

BENEFITS OF SEEING THE BIBLICAL HUMOR

There is also much to be gained. Out of his explorations Hershey H. Friedman notes, "There are many types of humor [in the Hebrew Bible]. These include: puns, wordplays, riddles, jokes, satires, lampoons, sarcasm, irony, wit, black humor, comedy, slapstick, farce, burlesques, caricatures, parody, and travesty."[4] When one comes to such conclusions about our scriptures there are important benefits:

- For one thing, we may enjoy reading and studying scripture more.
- In turn, this sense of delight and curiosity may influence how we interpret a passage. (If we recognize the "log in the eye" as a joke, our understanding might go in a different direction than a more labored analysis might take us.)
- Then, this may lead us to look for more examples of humor in our scriptures.
- And when this happens, it may further enhance our appreciation of the nature of scriptures.
- These discoveries may impact our biblical interpretation and methods of searching for the meaning of the text.

4. Friedman, *Humor in the Hebrew Bible*, 1.

- And, in turn, we may also be led to fresh ways to teach, study, and explore scripture with those we guide in these endeavors.
- This renewed experience of scripture might enrich our understanding of God, gospel, church, and ministry.
- Thus, if there is indeed widespread humor in scripture, it might lead us toward a beginning theology of humor.
- And, in turn, this discovery might invite / encourage engaging humor as an integral practice for doing and sustaining ministry.
- Even all this may be understating the benefits. There are distinguished biblical scholars who are finding humor as a key to unlock the meaning of scriptures. Some focus on the parables; others see a humorous perspective in the miracle stories—their unpredictability their challenge to persons' quest for power.[5]

It is indeed important to know of the presence of humor in Scripture. Further, this humor exists so abundantly that I will be able to provide only scattered representative examples.

HUMOR IN THE HEBREW SCRIPTURES

I have always loved the vivid and playful story telling of many parts of the Bible. These stories first awakened me to the humor of scriptures. Then it begins to dawn that I saw only the smallest part of what delighted me.

Out of years of in-depth study, J. William Whedbee offers this thesis: "[T]he Holy Book we call the Bible revels in a profoundly ambivalent laughter, a divine and human laughter that by turns is both mocking and joyous, subversive and celebrative, and finally a laughter that results in an exuberant and transformative comic vision."[6]

Comic structure

Whedbee sketches out the "anatomy of comedy" in the Bible and offers several examples. He finds this comedy structure repeated again and again. There are four basic elements in biblical comedy.

The first of these is the plotline. At the beginning there is a state of harmony and peace. This becomes challenged or threatened in some form. But as the action unfolds, the situation swings upward and hopeful toward the end. This may be described as the "U-shaped plot."

5. Donnelly, "Divine Folly," 389.

6. Whedbee, *The Bible and the Comic*, 4–5.

Second, there are basic personality types within the comedy which may be either human, or sometimes sub-human or animal (such as the serpent in Genesis 3). These types include buffoons, clowns, fools, simpletons, rogues, and tricksters. In comedy, the royal and the powerful may be undermined by portraying them as fools, or simpletons.

Third, comedy employs certain linguistic and stylistic strategies. There is a vast range of these strategies we mentioned including punning, wordplay, parody, hyperbole, redundancy, and repetitiousness. Further, comedy may include incongruity, irony, discrepancy, reversal, and surprise, perhaps moving into the ludicrous and ridiculous.

Fourth, comedy has a range of functions and intentions. This intent moves between conserving and subverting. It may support that which is seen as good, Godly, and wholesome in a society, or it may take dead aim at the repressive and tyrannical.[7]

After sketching out these components, this author goes on to explore "exemplary texts" where he points out which of these elements are employed and how they are utilized. His choices include the following:

- The comedy of creation (Genesis 1–11)
- Domestic comedy—the fathers and mothers of Israel as comic figures (Genesis 12–50)
- Humor in deliverance and liberation—the twin comedies of Exodus and Esther. Anyone who has had opportunity to take part in a Passover Seder knows something of the "comic celebration" of the Exodus story. He places beside it Esther, "as comic a story as has ever been told."[8] The Jewish celebration of Purim highlights this story with laughter and joy. (More on this a little later.)
- Jonah as a joke.
- The comedy of Job. He admits that his view of Job as comedy is a very small minority among scholars. Still, he points out that with the prologue and postlogue, it is a "U-shaped plot." He notes further that Job's "comforters" are caricatures of wise counselors and that Job's sarcastic and satirical rejection of his friends' irrelevant advice is "sharp, brilliant, and merited."
- And paradox and parody in the Song of Songs.

7. Ibid., 7–10.
8. Ibid., 171.

Example: Abraham and Sarah and descendents

We will pick just two passages he mentions for a closer look. The first is the story of Abraham and Sarah.[9] Chapters 12–21 of Genesis contain this story. It begins when God calls Abraham to leave his own country and kindred to a land God would show. God offers a promise "I will make of you a great nation, and I will bless you, and make your name great so that you will be a blessing." (12:2). Abraham obeys, but there is one catch and one exception. The catch is that Abraham—already a mature man—has no children. The exception is that he takes one kinsman along—his nephew, Lot. Possibly he saw Lot as a surrogate or adoptive son.

ALMOST: ANSWERS OF CHILDREN BEING TESTED ON INFORMATION FROM THE BIBLE

Adam and Eve were created from an apple tree. Noah's wife was Joan of Ark. Noah built an ark and the animals came on in pears.

Samson slayed the Philistines with the axe of the Apostles.

The Egyptians were all drowned in the dessert. Afterwards, Moses went up to Mount Cyanide to get the Ten Commandments.

Moses died before he ever reached Canada. Then Joshua led the Hebrews in the Battle of Geritol.

David was a Hebrew king who was skilled at playing the liar. He fought the Finkelstein's, a race of people who lived in Biblical times.

Solomon, one of David's sons, had 300 wives and 700 porcupines.

The Epistles were the wives of the Apostles.

One of the oppossums was St. Matthew who was also a taximan.

Christians have only one spouse. This is called monotony.

St. Paul cavorted to Christianity, he preached holy acrimony which is another name for marriage.

9. The text uses the names Abram and Sarai at the beginning and later changes them to Abraham and Sarah. For simplicity's sake, I will use one set of names in recalling this story.

As the story proceeds, there is both human failure and frustration. When forced to go to Egypt because of famine, Abraham portrays his beautiful wife as his sister for safety reasons. The frustration is that no children are born. Abraham and Sarah take various steps to try to solve this. First, he names as his heir Eliezer of Damascus (if Lot were the first choice as substitute son, that must not have worked out). Next Sarah has Abraham copulate with her Egyptian slave girl, Hagar. Though a son, Ishmael, is born from that union, he is not seen as the promised child either.

Finally, when Abraham is 99 and Sarah 90, God again promises a child, "Then Abraham fell on his face and laughed" (17:17). This must be some sort of cruel joke, the most ridiculous thing he ever heard.

In chapter 18, the Lord visits Abraham by the oaks of Mamre. After Abraham has provided hospitality and food (with Sarah eavesdropping from the tent) the Lord promises that in due season Sarah will have a child. This time it is Sarah's turn to laugh at such foolishness. "So Sarah laughed to herself . . . The Lord said to Abraham, 'Why did Sarah laugh?' . . . But Sarah denied saying, 'I did not laugh;' for she was afraid. He said, 'Oh yes, you did laugh'" (18:12, 13, 15).

When the child is indeed born, Sarah declares, "God has brought laughter for me; everyone who hears will laugh with me" (21:6). Fittingly, the son is named Isaac which means "laughter." The son of the father of a great nation was named Laughter. This leads Conrad Hyers to conclude, "The history of Israel begins—if this does not sound too impious—with a joke, a divine joke."[10] This laughter becomes the laughter of faith for generations to come.

The stories of the foreparents of Israel continue with equally engaging comedy. The subsequent accounts of Jacob, Esau, and Laban regale us with the adventures of tricksters and rogues. (For those who remember the old TV series, I think of these stories as "The Maverick brothers of the Bible.")

Indeed, one of the themes of Genesis is that "the one who deceives is ultimately in turn deceived"—a comedy of errors. Jacob deceived his nearly blind father Isaac to obtain a blessing. Laban in turn deceived Jacob, first giving him the wrong wife. Then Laban was the one deceived by Jacob and Rachel when they fled with his *terraphim* (statues used for idolatry or divination). Laban asked "Why have you stolen my gods?"

10. Hyers, *And God Created Laughter*, 10.

The Midrash notes it can't be much of a god if it can be stolen. There is also rough humor here in that his "gods" were under Rachel's posterior while she feigned "the manner of women."[11] This is found in Gen 21–33.

In turn, Jacob is deceived by his sons about their brother Joseph's supposed death, and then these brothers are deceived by Joseph. That final episode of Genesis, Joseph and his brothers is indeed a domestic comedy of sibling rivalry so fierce it repeatedly almost becomes a tragedy before the joyful and healing reconciliation. See Gen 35–50. (Tim Rice and Andrew Lloyd Webber's musical "Joseph and the Amazing Technicolor Dreamcoat" captures the playfulness, if not the divine dimension, of these narratives.)

Example: Jonah

The other passage we will explore is the book of Jonah, a strange presence among the 17 books of prophets. There is very little of what one finds in other books of the prophets. Instead there is disobedience and reversal. Some have observed that the prophet is not Jonah but the author of this book who wrote a profound, many dimensional comic masterpiece.

It begins with a play on words—"Jonah" means "dove," sometimes a symbol for the people of Israel. "Amittai" means faithfulness. So the first verse of Jonah reads (and this verse is in usual prophetic language) "Now the word of the LORD came to Dove, son of Faithfulness saying, 'Go at once to Nineveh . . ."

There the similarity ends. Unlike other prophetic books where the prophet resists and then obeys, Jonah sets out to flee over the sea in exactly the opposite direction. The book can be divided into two episodes: (1) Jonah's disobedience, which ends in God's mercy and deliverance for the sailors and Jonah (1:1—2:10); (2) Jonah's reluctant and repulsive obedience to God, which ends with God's mercy for the Ninevites—and for Jonah (3:1—4:11).

When Jonah arrives in Nineveh, his only message (cried out) is "Forty days and Nineveh shall be overthrown!"(3:4b). But, they repent! This leads Hyers to comment, "The world's shortest and poorest sermon becomes the world's most successful sermon."[12] How is this for parody—"The reluctant Jonah accomplished in five words what numerous elo-

11. Friedman, *Humor in the Hebrew Bible*, 6 of 24.

12. Hyers, *And God Created Laughter*, 104.

quent prophets could not accomplish in thousands of words and all this without even trying."[13]

The success of the campaign does not please Jonah. He asks God to die, "I knew that you are a gracious God and merciful, slow to anger and abounding in steadfast love, and ready to relent from punishing" (4:2b). Whereupon God playfully provides Jonah a bush (possibly a castor bean plant) overnight for his comfort, and then takes it away and engages in a bit of gentle repartee with him.

This little book is filled with over and understatement, surprise, opposite reaction, inconsistency, and absurdity. Many scholars recognize its comic quality and variously classify it parody or satire or comic novella. Clearly it is both a literary masterpiece and a profound religious vision—if there is room within God's care for sailors, Ninevites, and Jonah, there must be a place for even us!

Other forms of biblical humor

We now move on from those textual examples to more specific examination and examples of several of the forms of humor to which we have alluded up to now.

The Bible contains numerous *wordplays*, *double entendres*, and *puns*. The Hebrew Bible in its original language contained neither vowels, nor punctuation. A word written without vowels can often be read in any number of ways. This leads to some delightful puns and other plays on words

> NOT ONLY PUNS IN THE BIBLE, BUT PUNS ABOUT THE BIBLE—WHERE IN THE BIBLE DO YOU FIND:
>
> - Baseball? "In the big inning . . . Eve stole first and Adam stole second.
> - Tennis? "Joseph served in the courts of Pharaoh."
> - Foreign cars? "They were all together in one Accord."
> - The old maid's favorite verse? "I will not have you, ignorant brethren."
> - Why the Romans had to shut down the Coliseum? The lions were eating up all the prophets.

13. Friedman, *Humor in the Hebrew Bible*, 21 of 24.

that rabbinic studies of scripture have long noted. Here is a tiny sampling of some of those.

The name "Adam" is formed from the word for "earth" or "clay" (something like a human out of the humus). The name "Eve" translates "she who makes live," a fitting name for the mother of the human race. Nearly all Hebrew personal and place names are associated with puns—some clear and some strained. When Eve says at the birth of a son, "I have made a man from the Lord," Cain's name is from the word "made." When God splits up the conspirators by confounding their language, the Hebrew word for confuse is similar to the name "Babel" and in turn is the origin for the English word "babble." Whedbee has noted ". . . puns are jokes embedded in inventive word-play . . ."[14] Biblical puns indeed often contain a smile or chuckle as well as a significant truth.

There are plays on words in people's names as well. Indeed, the Talmud suggests some names in the Hebrew Bible are not real names, but "made up" to symbolize—and perhaps poke fun at—these characters. For example "Nimrod" (Gen 10:8–10) who led rebellion sounds like the Hebrew word for rebel, *morod*. The name Balaam signifies *balah am* (he destroyed the people). Delilah is similar to *dildalah*, (weakened) and indeed she weakened Samson's heart, strength, and deeds. Korah (a leader of rebellion in Num 16) has a name that resembles the Hebrew word *karchah* which means baldness. The opinion is offered that he was called that because he created baldness (defoliation) in Israel.[15]

Further, within the Bible there is *witty repartee and bargaining* between a human being and God. Abraham bargains God down to agreeing not to destroy Sodom if ten righteous men can be found there. The session began with asking God to spare the city if fifty righteous men can be found! (Gen 18:23–33).

There are a number of such exchanges between Moses and God, first answering his resistance to his call (Exod 4:10–17) and then, time and again, while Moses was leading the Israelites. In Exodus 33:12–16, Moses outwits God by using God's previous promises to him to elicit a new and renewed assurance. And in Numbers 14:13–16, Moses dissuades God from destroying the people by pointing out what the neigh-

14. Whedbee, *The Bible and the Comic*, 29.

15. Friedman, *Humor in the Hebrew Bible*, 16–24. These are just a few of the examples he cites. This is one of the aspects of biblical humor where knowledge of the language is needed to note and appreciate the many times it is used.

boring nations will think of a God who could not bring God's people to the place promised!

In the rabbinical tradition, it is told that Moses once took God to task for using inconsistent pronouns! In Exodus 3:10, God calls Moses to "bring forth my people, the Israelites out of Egypt." But when they sin with the golden calf, God tells Moses, ". . .your people, whom you have brought out of the land of Egypt have corrupted themselves." (Exod 32:7). It is said that Moses then protested, "Wait a minute, God. You can't call them your people when they're good and my people when they're bad." The rabbis concluded that God broke into laughter at that moment, enjoying the prayerful teasing of God's beloved and chosen leader.[16]

There is in all of this an audacity, a chutzpah, and a lovely witty relationship with the divine—echoed in Tevyah's conversations with God in the musical *Fiddler on the Roof.*

Another form of humor in scriptures is the *riddle*. The most famous riddle in scripture is found in Judges 14, where Samson finds a beehive filled with honey inside a lion he had killed. His riddle to the Philistines was, "Out of the eater came something to eat. Out of the strong came something sweet." (Judges 14:14). Fisher points out that there is a pun here that would have made the riddle solvable. In a rare usage, the word '*ari* can mean both lion and honey. As he points out, if they were clever enough, they could have solved it without cheating.[17]

Still another frequently used type of humor in the Bible is *exaggeration*. One example is the series of complaints brought to Moses in the desert. For example, "We remember the fish we used to eat in Egypt for nothing, the cucumbers, the melons, the leeks, the onions, and the garlic . . ." (Num 11:5) Fish served them free? Yes,—except of course for the long hours of back-breaking labor and the murder of their children!

Other exaggerations are found in the book of Proverbs. In this book there are lampoons of fools, lazy people, and quarrelsome women—all of them with exaggerated and comical caricatures. For example, Proverbs 11:22, "Like a gold ring in a wine's snout is a beautiful woman without discretion." Or 26:17, "He who meddles in a quarrel not his own is like one who takes a passing dog by the ears." Or 26:18–19, "Like a madman who throws firebrands, arrows, and death is a man who deceives

16. Taylor, "A Theology of Humor," 3.

17. Several of these examples of biblical humor were from the essay by Fisher, "The Divine Comedy," 574–79.

his neighbor and says, 'I am only joking!'" Taking these together, there seems to be a subtext to use humor but do not be careless with it.

Still another type of exaggeration is the element of surprise imagery. For example within the beautiful and romantic Song of Solomon, there are some amazingly strange (and playful?) images. The writer compares his love to a mare in Pharaoh's chariots (1:9). He goes on to say her hair is like a flock of goats trailing down from Mt. Gilead; her teeth like a flock of ewes (4:1–2), and her nose like the tower of Lebanon which overlooks Damascus (7:5). What maiden could resist such "romantic" descriptions?[18]

Yet another form of biblical humor is the *fable*. For example, in Num 22:21–35, there is Balaam's talking ass, which would not move at the sight of an angel and resisted in spite of repeated beatings. Not only does the donkey talk, but speaks like an intelligent and eloquent individual. The donkey asks "Am I not your donkey, which you have ridden all your life to this day? Have I been in the habit of treating you this way?" (Num 22:30) Indeed the donkey seems to possess a reasonable, intelligent, and patient outlook—much more than its owner! Also, there is Jotham's fable about the trees choosing a ruler, and by default choosing the thorn bush to be their king. (Judges 9:7–15)[19]

A rather widespread form of biblical humor is *satire* and *irony*. These show up in a variety of related forms. What is the difference between these two terms? Ze'ev Weisman suggests that the difference is in mood and tone. He notes that in irony there is more a mood of forgiveness. There might be a loving, respectful recognition of the quirks and foibles of the human race or a particular part of it. On the other hand, in satire, "the dominant tone is that of animosity and the insult. Satire exploits rhetoric for its political purposes. It is polemical in its very nature."[20] While this is a helpful distinction, it must also be noted that satire and irony often blend into each other or overlap with each other. And even when they do not, sometimes they are hard to distinguish.

Friedman points out that the very foundation and structure of the book of Esther is steeped in irony. During a marathon feast, King Ahasuerus commands seven eunuchs to "bring Queen Vashti before the king wearing [only?] the royal crown, in order to show the people and the officials her beauty . . ." (Esth 1:10-11). The ironies are many: one

18. Friedman, *Humor in the Hebrew Bible*, 17–18.

19. Greenstein, "Humor and Wit," 330–32.

20. Weisman, *Political Satire in the Bible*, 8.

queen refuses an order and is deposed, while the next one violates protocol and enters the king's inner court unsummoned; Haman suggests an honor he expects to be conferred on him, but instead must confer it on his enemy Mordecai; then Haman erects a gallows for Mordecai and is hanged on it himself. The individuals on top at the beginning of the book are at their lowest point at the book's conclusion and vice versa.[21]

Satire can take any number of forms. There is *sarcasm*. In Genesis 37:19, Joseph's brothers comment, "Here comes the dreamer," literally the "master of dreams." In Amos 4:4–5, Amos proclaims, "Come to Bethel, and transgress; to Gilgal and multiply transgressions; bring your sacrifices every morning, your tithes every three days, . . . for so you love to do, O people of Israel." Even God engages in sarcasm with Job, "Where were you when I laid the foundation of the earth?" (Job 38:4) When you can create a world, then you can advise me on how to run mine!

It may take the form of *ridicule*. One of the clearest examples is Elijah's taunts and mockery of the prophets of Baal when they are trying to call down fire on their sacrifice,

1 Kings 18:27, "Cry aloud for he is a god; either he is musing, or he is gone aside [perhaps a euphemism for going to the toilet], or he is on a journey, or perhaps he is asleep and must be wakened" (RSV). Another statement of ridicule—Isaiah 44:9–17, Isaiah describes a person cutting down a tree, burning part of it and making an idol with part of it. "Half of it he burns in the fire . . . roasts meat . . . and is satisfied . . . The rest of it he makes into a god, his idol, bows down to it and worships it; he prays to it and says, 'Save me, for you are my god!'"

For a people who were conquered, occupied, and exiled for so much of their life, it is not hard to see why there would be much satire and irony. Political opposition as well as perspective on the fragile human condition are all included here. It is also to be noted that this was not only exercised upon foreign rulers, but also upon themselves, their rulers, religious leaders, and the way they lived their lives.

And even as we note the strong strain of satire and humor, we also recall the twofold thrust of biblical humor. Not only does it subvert, challenge, and reveal, it also "sympathizes, celebrates, accepts, confirms, and embraces." There is not only an opposition to all that is unworthy, there is a robust affirmation of life. In biblical humor we are called into question, but we are also given hope, strength, and joy.[22]

21. Friedman, *Humor in the Hebrew Bible*, 8–9.

22. Whedbee, *The Bible and the Comic*, 178–288.

HUMOR IN THE NEW TESTAMENT

In the New Testament, the humor continues and extends these basic purposes, styles and themes. These purposes and themes are both focused more closely and expanded more broadly in the central events of which the New Testament speaks.

More Answers from those kids taking Bible tests at a parochial School

Lot's wife was a pillar of salt during the day, but a ball of fire during the night.

Samson was a strongman who let himself be led astray by a Jezebel like Delilah.

The first commandment was when Eve told Adam to eat the apple.

The seventh commandment is thou shalt not admit adultery.

The greatest miracle in the Bible is when Joshua told his son to stand still and he obeyed him.

When Mary heard she was the mother of Jesus, she sang the magna carta.

When the three wise guys from the east side arrived they found Jesus in the manager.

Jesus was born because Mary had an immaculate contraption.

Jesus enunciated the golden rule which says to do unto others before they do one to you. He also explained a man doth not live by sweat alone.

R. Alan Culpepper finds similar strains of humor to that which his colleagues found in the Hebrew Bible. He points out that, "A foundational incongruity sustains the New Testament. God enters the world as a baby born to a peasant girl, is unrecognized by all but a few, and redeems the world by dying on a cross. Rejecting wisdom and signs, God chose to save those who believe through the foolishness of preaching."[23]

Humorous understandings of Jesus' nature

Over and again, the New Testament writers express wonder at God's working in humble and unexpected ways in Jesus of Bethlehem and

23. Culpeppper, "Humor and Wit," 333.

Nazareth. These amazing surprises fill them with comic delight. Jesus himself is "the comic surprise (or divine incongruity) we call the incarnation."[24]

This is seen in the stories of his birth. We need to scrape through all the sacred and secular overlays, and hear these narratives again as if for the first time, if we are to experience this. As Hyers notes, "In some mysterious way, in an infant born to a poor peasant girl in a donkey shed in a small, remote town in a minor province among a conquered people of no particular importance, God was specially present. Emmanuel, God with us. What divine foolishness is this?" All the glorious contradictions of his life are here—royal birth and nowhere to lay his head; descendent of the great King David and born in an animal shed. "Above is a brilliant star and angelic chorus; beneath is straw and dirt and the smell of manure."[25]

The birth story of the promised one reads like a game of "hide and go seek" or "peek-a-boo" or like a "Jack-in-the-box." Now you see it, now you don't. The people who should know about him don't; the weak and humble who should not know are told. Wise men look in the wrong places, and then find him, just for an instant. When others come looking, he is nowhere to be found.

Furthermore, this amazement about Jesus is seen in his heritage as described by Matthew's genealogy (Matt 1:1–16), that traces his family tree for generations. As Doug Adams humorously notes, not only is there a prostitute (Rahab, v.5) in Jesus' family tree, there are two other sexual scandals. Judah, mistaking his disguised widowed daughter-in-law Tamar for a prostitute, consorts with and impregnates her (v.3). David adulterously seduces the beautiful "wife of Uriah" (v.6) and then has him killed.

Furthermore, out of the other names in this genealogy, one third are—as the Bible describes them—evil kings, and a third are unknown entities. Adams notes that if God could bring forth a Jesus from out of that mess, there is hope for our children![26]

As deep a mystery as Jesus' nature arising in these humble and sordid circumstances, an even more profound mystery is why such a person had to suffer a shameful and painful death on a cross. He was the very

24. Donnelly, "Divine Folly," 389.

25. Hyers, *And God Created Laughter*, 54, 62.

26. Adams, *The Prostitute in the Family Tree*, 2–5.

embodiment of divine love and he suffered a cruel, criminal's death. Only in the light of glorious resurrection and further reflection were followers able to speak of the foolishness of the cross. The darkest time in human history, prompted by the evil influence of corrupted human nature—in religion, in political leaders, in military personnel—was, nonetheless, used by God to achieve God's redemptive purposes. With eyes of faith, the Jesus story is seen to have surprising endings, at first tragic and then gloriously triumphant.

A further insight into the comic mystery of this Jesus is provided as we see how the gospel writers frame their telling of the Jesus story.

- Mathew begins by telling of magi who came *from the nations* and ends with the risen, authority filled Jesus sending disciples *to the nations* to make disciples, teach, and baptize.
- Mark opens his gospel with an adult Jesus (after baptism and temptation) quickly at work, calling, healing, and preaching. Mark closes (16:8, original ending) with the disciples still puzzled about a possible resurrection and with Jesus' work to do, to carry on what he began.
- Luke opens with angels proclaiming and singing of Jesus' birth—descent to a specific place and family, and it closes with his ascent (soon to be followed by Pentecost), continuing his power through the early church into all the earth.
- In John, Jesus' first act is to provide wine for a wedding feast, and his last act is to cook a breakfast for confused disciples, restoring them to faith and mission.

These are all "U shaped comedy plots." Truly this person is the embodiment of, as well as the carrier of, many of God's unexpected and surprising gifts.

Jesus' use of humor

The joy is magnified in that Jesus performed his ministry engaging multiple forms of humor. This may be seen in a number of ways. One was his *love of children*. He objected when people tried to keep children away from him. As Mark (10:16) vividly tells it, "He took them up in his arms, laid his hands on them, and blessed them." Blessed them—made them laugh? That is not hard to do, Someone has observed that children laugh, on the average, 400 times a day; adults by contrast laugh an average of

15 times a day. Perhaps some of the things he loved about children were their candor, their fresh look at things, their laughter, and their delight in play. In his teachings, he spoke of children's games. He also took a child and told his disciples to become like this child. Indeed, he said the childlike spirit was the only way into his kingdom of love.

Still another part his humor is the *striking statement*, the *hyperbole*. Trueblood terms this method "the preposterous." When Carl Burke was working with street kids and they sometimes translated Jesus' words into their language, they called these statements "gassers." Among these "gassers" was his contention "It is easier for a camel to go through the eye of a needle than for a rich man to enter the kingdom of God." (Mark 10:25). People must have chuckled, gasped, choked on that. But then, after the scandal of his statement had sunk in, with exquisite timing, he added the punch line, "[However] for God all things are possible." (Mark 10:27). In one of his stories, Jesus told of a man in debt to his employer for millions of dollars, who had the debt forgiven but then in turn would not let go a fellow servant's debt of twenty dollars. (Matt 18:23–35). With such a striking statement, people would guffaw and be ready for the suggestion, "When you have been forgiven so much, shouldn't you forgive, at least a little?"

A bedrock part of Jesus' humor was *story / parable*. Douglas Adams points that biblical stories, including many of Jesus' parables are like "grandparent stories." "Parents tend to clean up their stories; grandparents tell stories that are more truthful and have many rough edges . . . grandparent stories are humorous and give hope and life by sharing a reality similar to our own." The rough edges in biblical stories may include unethical or ambiguous characters, unresolved issues, and surprise endings. Biblical stories, including Jesus' parables are "mirrors for identity and not models for morality."[27] Adams points out further that many parables don't end but are rather like an episode of a soap opera. For example at the end of the telling of the so-called "Parable of the Prodigal Son," the father and the elder brother are outside arguing! All of this suggests that the original parables involved a much more lively interchange than we usually imagine, and this is a dialogue / exploration that can continue with us in the present.

In some of Jesus' parables, very little imagination is needed to find the humor. He told about a poor widow who needed justice in a court

27. Ibid., 1, 6.

ruling. Lacking the money to "influence" the judge, she simply came night and day to the judge, calling out for justice at every quiet moment in his court. Finally she wore him out with her persistence. The judge concluded, "Though I have no fear of God and no respect for anyone, yet because this widow keeps bothering me, I will grant her justice so that she may not wear me out by continually coming" (Luke 18:4–5). Luther is said to have translated the judge's speech, "I will grant her justice, lest she deafen me."

Jesus also told about a man and his family all cuddled for a night's rest in their large family bed on the floor. At midnight, a desperate neighbor rattles the door and pleads for their leftover bread to feed a guest. He rattles and rattles and rattles until the one in bed gets up and gives him "whatever he needs" (Luke 11:5–9). Both these stories would have drawn smiles and chuckles, preparing them to hear Jesus speak to them about prayer.

Another form of Jesus' humor is *repartee and playful dialogue*. His conversation with the Samaritan woman at the well has elements of this, especially when he says, "Go call your husband."

"I have no husband."

"You are right . . ." (John 4:16–17). There was another conversation, this one with a Syrophoenician woman's request for healing for her child. When Jesus resisted, saying, ". . . it is not fair to take the children's food and throw it to the dogs," with on-the-target wit, she came back, "Sir, even the dogs under the table eat the children's crumbs."(Mark 7:27b–28) Jesus was touched and probably amused, and he responded favorably to her urgent request. There is also an amusing conversation, mostly about Jesus, in John 9, when a healed man born blind has repeated, conflicted conversations with religious authorities, raising the question in an ironical way who is blind and who sees, and what do the sighted see (or fail to see) that is true?

Doug Adams also points to the humorous repartee in another event to which biblical commentators give great weight and ponder deeply. Humor makes a difference in how we interpret this passage. In Matthew 22:15–22 Jesus is challenged by members of another religious party within the Judaism of his day (Pharisees). While many read this passage as separating faith from politics, they may miss Jesus' sharp humor in slipping out of a trap being laid for him. When he is asked about paying taxes to Caesar, Jesus asks his questioners to produce a coin. They do so, even though a strictly pious Jew would not carry a coin bearing Caesar's image and an inscription proclaiming him king and God. By producing the coin in question, they have embarrassed themselves and incriminated themselves of breaking two commandments. After Jesus tells them to give Caesar what is Caesar's, "and render to God the things

Humor About the Ark

Somehow Noah and the Ark seems to hit some comics' funny bones. There's Bill Cosby's classic comedy routine about the supposed conversation between God and Noah:

> God: Noah, I want you to build an ark.
> Noah:Right. What's an ark?
> God: Build it 80 by 40 by 30 cubits.
> Noah: Right. What's a cubit?
> God: Let's see, I used to know . . .

(See / hear a couple different versions on http://wwwyoutube.com. Write "Cosby" and then look for the Noah episodes.)

Or, there's 'Everything I need to know about life, I learned from Noah's Ark:'

1: Don't miss the boat.
2: Remember that we are all in the same boat.
3: Plan ahead. It wasn't raining when Noah built the Ark.
4: Stay fit. When you're 600-years-old, someone may ask you to do something really big.
5: Don't listen to critics; just get on with the job that needs to be done.
6: Build your future on high ground.
7: For safety's sake, travel in pairs.
8: Speed isn't always an advantage. The snails were on board with the cheetahs.
9: When you're stressed, float a while.
10: Remember, the Ark was built by amateurs; the Titanic by professionals.
11: No matter the storm, when you are with God, there's always a rainbow waiting.

(This item was taken from an email.)

that are God's"—there is no indication he returned the coin to them. Perhaps he pocketed it and had the last laugh![28]

One more method in Jesus' humor is that he also employed *irony* and quite possibly *satire*. This is the humor that reveals our mistakes and our frailties. Elton Trueblood wrote, "Humor . . . can lead to the unmasking of error and thereby, the emergence of truth." In this connection, he quoted Aristotle, "No society is in good health without laughing at itself quietly and privately; no character is sound without self-scrutiny, without turning inward to see where it may have overreached itself."[29] In a more earthy way, someone has written, "Humor is the hole that lets the sawdust out of a stuffed shirt."

Jesus clearly engaged irony. In speaking of his intra-religious antagonists, the Pharisees, he likened them to a person scrubbing away at a cup, getting it spotless—but on the outside only, leaving the inside dirty. Then the person tries to drink from this cup, carefully straining the water so the gnats will not be drunk. But in this carefulness, the person winds up swallowing the camel on which one is riding instead! He describes a person carefully tithing a plant or two from one's herb garden, but forgetting "justice, mercy, and faith." (Matt 23:23–26).

Are these statements irony—wistful noting and forgiving of human weakness? Or are they satire—with intent of defeating the opposition? Both of these statements are part of a long chapter of "woes" Jesus pronounces on scribes and Pharisees. At the end of this same chapter is Jesus' lament over Jerusalem. "How often have I desired to gather your children together as a hen gathers her brood under her wings." (Matt 23:37b). There is rigorous critique and longing for reconciliation, side by side. My hunch is that the first time Jesus uttered such statements they were irony, perhaps playful irony. However, as the conflict grew, in the face of intractable resistance, these words became satire to expose and confront the influence of leaders hardened in opposition to him.

The One that God sent also engages a wide ranging humor as one method of communicating his message and mission. Those who hear and believe respond with joy and healing.

We conclude this survey with examples of humor in other parts of the New Testament.

28. Donnelly, "Divine Folly," 389–90. She is reporting / summarizing Adams "Bringing Biblical Humor to Life in Liturgy."

29. Trueblood, *The Humor of Christ*, 53, 54.

Humor in Acts

Certainly there is humor, rivaling slapstick humor in Acts 12. Peter is in prison chained to two guards. Believers are gathered in a house praying for his release. An angel releases Peter and sends him out, and he goes to the house where they are praying. He knocks at the door. A servant girl, Rhoda answers. She is so shocked and overjoyed, that rather than letting him in, she leaves him behind and rushes in to tell the others that Peter is at the door. They say to her, "You are out of your mind!" (Acts 12:15). You can't make up stuff like that!

And why would the story of Eutychus be included if not for comic relief? This was the young man who "began to fall into a deep sleep while Paul talked still longer." (Acts 20:9). In his sleep he fell three floors and was thought to be dead. Paul took him in his arms and affirmed life was still in him. They took the boy away, but Paul went back up stairs "and continued to converse with them until dawn." (20:11)

Humor in Paul's Writings

Doug Adams sees humor in Paul's correspondence with the Corinthians. Perhaps they thought a bit too highly of themselves. Further, they indulged in cliques and divisiveness, and moral laxness as well. In Adams' parlance, they needed "grandma letters" with all the rough edges to help them be the church Christ intends. To do so, Paul offers a healthy dose of varied irony to them.

- He minimizes his own importance. "Has Christ been divided? Was Paul crucified for you? I thank God I baptized none of you except . . ." (1 Cor 1:13–14).
- He further relates what Adams calls an "antiautobiography"—that is a self-story that contains none of the usual accomplishments one usually includes, but rather tells of his struggles and humiliations (2 Cor 11).
- To reveal how silly and damaging their self-importance is, he constructs a parody with body parts talking to each other (1 Cor. 12:12–27).

- When he finally gets around to all their divisive questions on which they would like him to take sides, he invariably responds with "both . . . and . . ." answers.[30]

Humor sustains individuals and communities in their daily struggles. But there is even greater wonder.

It is this—" . . . we proclaim Christ crucified, a stumbling block to Jews and foolishness [a favorite term of Paul's, by the way] to Gentiles, but to those who are called, both Jews and Greeks, Christ the power of God and the wisdom of God. For God's foolishness [that term again] is wiser than human wisdom, and God's weakness is stronger than human strength." (1 Cor. 1:23–25). And the wonder is that God is not defeated but will triumph "in the fullness of time." (Eph 1:10). Furthermore, the wonder is this, "I am confident of this, that the one who began a good work among you will bring it to completion by the day of Jesus Christ." (Phil 1:6).

We serve a surprising God who acted in amazing ways through a joy filled Redeemer and Lord and whose story is still unfolding. Let us laugh and rejoice. That is a perspective worth having!

QUESTIONS FOR PERSONAL AND GROUP REFLECTION

1. What is your heritage as regards humor in the scriptures? In what ways do you affirm that heritage? Where do you evaluate that heritage and see humor in scriptures that others might have missed?
2. What in the Bible amuses you? What did this chapter fail to mention about biblical humor?
3. What was your opinion about humor in scripture before you read this chapter? What is it now? In what ways, if any, has it changed?
4. At what points did you find this chapter convincing? At what points did you feel it overstated a point of view or misinterpreted a Bible passage? Were there points where this chapter offended you? If so, where?
5. In this chapter, I share that this interpretation matters to me and means a great deal to me. How about you? In what ways, if any, does the point of view of this chapter matter to you? What impact

30. Adams, *The Prostitute in the Family Tree*, 78–97.

does it have on your biblical preaching and teaching and on the ministry and services you render?

6. What is the impact of this chapter's findings on the thesis of this book—that humor and play deserve to be a spiritual practice?

5

The Ultimate Comedian and the Rather Dull Crowd

(Toward a Theology and Ethic of Humor)

God is like a comedian playing to an audience that is afraid to laugh.

—Voltaire[1]

If you're not allowed to laugh in heaven, I don't want to go there.

—Martin Luther[2]

We now walk deeper into our consideration of humor as a spiritual practice. Out of our journey into the Bible, new questions emerge. Does God have a sense of humor? If so, where is it seen and experienced? Is our innate humor some aspect of our being in God's image? Are our play, laughter, comedy, and humor pleasing to God, a way to relate to God? Is some of it pleasing to God and some of it not? In the light of these questions, what is the claim and promise of humor on those who serve God's church?

In engaging these questions, we attempt a theology of humor and the ethic that responds to it. This is a daunting task to be approached humbly! The great Karl Barth called theology "a joyful science," but in all

1. Quoted in Goodheart, *Laughter Therapy*, 26.
2. Peter, *Peter's Quotations*, 286.

his brilliance and profundity, he also recognized even his limits. He once wrote, "The angels laugh at old Karl. They laugh at him because he tries to grasp the truth about God in a book of Dogmatics. They laugh at the fact that volume follows volume and each is thicker than the previous ones. As they laugh, they say to one another, 'Look! Here he comes now with his little pushcart full of volumes of the *Dogmatics!*'"[3] How much more must the angels be laughing at "old Dick," a much smaller theological mind, trying to probe the ways of God and humanity as regards humor!

AN INTRIGUING METAPHOR

When we speak of God's laughter we are using the theological method of analogy or metaphor. And since any image / metaphor can only take one part way, Barbara Bowe has wisely suggested, "Multiply your metaphors."

She mentions that in Islam, Muslims pray fingering a small set of beads while reciting the ninety-nine names of Allah. This practice leads to praying persons being surrounded with a profound sense of their deity's mysterious and multifaceted nature. Some of their prayer would include these names, "the Subtle One, the Compassionate, the All Forgiving, the Guide . . ." Thus this practice affords a wide array of ways to speak of God, each one offering a significant dimension which in turn needs to be supplemented by other terms.

Bowe goes on to point out that the Bible helps us with this by providing a vast array of metaphors for God. Within its pages are male, female, family, political, craftsperson, professional, animal, and inanimate metaphors for the divine one. She encourages enriching spirituality and theology by identifying, naming, reflecting on, praying on these many images—multiplying our metaphors. Indeed, she lists more than thirty biblical metaphors as aids to knowing the God beyond all names.[4]

We can benefit from her suggestion and carry it a step further by adding one more metaphor—God the humorist, the laughing God. If this image is accurate and faithful, we move a good distance toward the spiritual practice of humor and play we are considering. On occasion the

3. Quoted in Hyers, *The Comic Vision*, 55.

4. Bowe, *Biblical Foundations of Spirituality*, 27–30.

Bible uses this metaphor directly and in many other instances implies it. And yet, engaging this image raises still other questions.

How significant should this metaphor of a Laughing God be in our theology? Is it simply an asterisk or footnote, peripheral, rarely noticed and seldom referred to? And is that where it belongs?

Or is this vitally important—significant, not only in itself, but for its influencing and adding nuance to other metaphors for God? If we follow the scholars who are saying that humor is a key to understanding scripture, is humor also a key to understanding God? One of those scholars, Hershey H. Friedman, asserts, "Humor brings God closer to humankind."[5]

What is a faithful interpretation of God's laughter? Heresy is often not some new teaching. Rather, it is an overemphasis on some aspect of the historic faith to the neglect or minimizing of other equally significant aspects of the faith. We need to be aware of this possibility as regards a theology of humor.

Which would be the greater heresy? Would it be an overemphasis on God's humor to the neglect of other divine characteristics? Or would it be a neglect of divine laughter while strongly emphasizing God's holiness, righteousness, and judgment? One would be a rather shallow theology, while the other would lose much of what makes our faith a satisfying world view. Certainly some combination is ultimately more adequate and helpful.

It must be acknowledged that there is a sturdy part of our Christian tradition that rejects humor as part of the life of faith. In the year 390, the saintly Chrysostom preached against laughter and playfulness, seeing them as too close to paganism. In that sermon he said, "This world is not a theatre in which we can laugh; and we are not assembled together in order to burst into peals of laughter, but to weep for our sins." In the 17th century, Quaker Robert Barclay stated that Christians should avoid everything that does not suggest the utmost seriousness and fear of God. "For laughing, sporting, gaming, mocking, jesting, vain talking, is not Christian liberty, nor harmless mirth." Conrad Hyers who offered these quotes added, "According to such a definition, a truly 'divine' Christian ought to look something like a cross between a sour lemon and a dried prune."[6]

5. Friedman, "Humor in the Hebrew Bible," 285.

6. Hyers, *And God Created Laughter*, 26–27.

Even today, there is wide difference of opinion about how much humor is fitting, and where it should be allowed in Christian churches. One of my friends recalls being invited to preach in a church that was of a kindred denomination to his own. He told jokes in part of his sermon, and sensed he was being shunned afterward for doing so.

If a faithful theology of laughter avoids both extremes, where is the balance? In an essay, "Humor and Faith," Reinhold Niebuhr, one of the greatest theologians of the twentieth century, suggested that humor had a vital but extremely minor role. In an oft quoted statement, he summarized:

"Insofar as the sense of humor is recognition of incongruity, it is more profound than any philosophy which seeks to devour incongruity in reason. But the sense of humor remains healthy only when it deals with immediate issues and faces the obvious and surface irrationalities. It must move toward faith or sink into despair when the ultimate issues are raised.

"That is why there is laughter in the vestibule of the temple, the echo of laughter in the temple itself, but only faith and prayer, and no laughter, in the holy of holies."[7]

On the other hand, another theologian, Frederick Buechner, muses:

"Is it possible, I wonder, to say that it is only when you hear the Gospel as a wild and marvelous joke that you really hear it at all? Heard as anything else, the Gospel is the church's thing, the preacher's thing, the lecturer's thing. Heard as a joke—high and unbidden and ringing with laughter—it can only be God's thing."[8]

Buechner's statement resonates with the Apostle Paul's speaking of "God's foolishness" (1 Cor 1:25) that we noted in the previous chapter.

Though they reject the "no humor" stance of some of our forbearers, the statements of two fine theologians, "no laughter in the holy of holies" and "only when you hear the gospel as a wild and marvelous joke . . . you really hear it at all" seem to pull against each other. Clearly, I lean one way on that debate. I believe that Niebuhr was speaking of only one type of humor (ironical and analytic) and his conclusion should not be applied to all types. However, we will not at this time attempt to mediate

7. Niebuhr, "Humor and Faith," 130–31.

8. Buechner, *Telling the Truth*, 68.

that tension. Rather we will be aware of it as we continue to explore a theology and ethic of humor.

A SCHEMA OF DIVINE HUMOR

As we seek clarity on this issue, we will look at the Bible from yet another perspective. Within scriptures there is a threefold schema for a theology of laughter.[9]

Laughter of Creation

There is God's humor and laughter in God's creation. As the creation story tells us, "God saw that it was good." (Gen 1:12). The contemplation of all God has made moves us creatures to wonder, "When I look at your heavens, the work of your fingers, the moon and the stars that you have established; what are human beings that you are mindful of them . . . ?" (Ps 8:3–4a).

Furthermore, creation itself rejoices in being created. When created, "the morning stars sang together and all the heavenly beings shouted for joy." (Job 38:7). As creation renews itself every spring, ". . . you shall go out in joy and be led back in peace; the mountains and the hills before you shall burst into song, and all the trees of the field shall clap their hands." (Isa 55:12). It is a world that delights in its Creator and responds. Indeed mountains skip like rams and hills skip like lambs. (Ps 114:4, 6).

The humor of creation is seen in penguins, donkeys, zebras, monkeys, bullfrogs, and giraffes. Or as the Almighty One, speaking out of the whirlwind, reminds Job—ostriches. "The ostrich's wings flap wildly though its pinions lack plumage. For it leaves its eggs to the earth and lets them be warmed on the ground . . . When it spreads its plumes aloft, it laughs at the horse and its rider." (Job 39:13–14, 18). In the same speeches, the Lord twits Job in his limited humanity in the face of the mysterious and powerful creature, Leviathan. "Can you draw out Leviathan with a fishhook . . .? Will you play with it as a bird, or will you put it on a leash for your girls?" (Job 41:1, 5).

9. George Arthur Buttrick offered the threefold schema we will follow in "God and Laughter," 51–57. In a slightly different form, Conrad Hyers speaks of the three levels of humor (Paradise, Paradise Lost, Paradise Regained) in his book, *The Comic Vision and the Christian Faith*. Indeed, this schema is simply a restatement of classical Christian theology from the angle of humor.

A child seeing a camel for the first time exclaimed, "I don't believe it." The beauty and lavishness of creation is seen in foliage, flowers, and birds, all with their extravagant varieties of colors and forms, and waterfalls.

We are drawn to zoos and arboretums to be near God's lavish humor in all these things, even as we know creation did it better in their original settings, and we hope for freedom to move and good care for God's creatures we watch. We love the outdoors, whether our own backyard or magnificent parks, for there is something original, joyous, real to which we are attracted in God's creation.

Creation is not an unambiguous blessing. There is danger, hazard, and sometimes tragedy there as well. Still, in the basic laughter of creation, deep calls unto deep.

Laughter of derision

Further, God's laughter is heard when we humans forget or ignore our place in creation and try to usurp another's. In the Bible, this is where God's laughter is explicitly mentioned at all. "He who sits in the heavens laughs; the LORD has them in derision." (Ps 2:4). Also, "The wicked plot against the righteous and gnash their teeth at them; but the LORD laughs at the wicked, for he sees that their day is coming." (Ps 37:12–13). And again, "But you laugh at them, O LORD; you hold all the nations in derision." (Ps 59:8).

> God's plan made a hopeful beginning,
> But we spoiled our chances by sinning.
> I trust that the story
> will end in God's glory,
> But right now, the other side's winning.

While we first might be delighted to hear scriptures speak of God's laughter, we are chastened when that laughter is an expression of disdain for human pretension and wickedness! Could it be that this laughter is one aspect of divine pity and care? We are promised that God "has compassion for those who fear him" as does a father for his children. For this God "knows how we were made" and "remembers we are dust." (Ps 103:13–14).

This compassion / derision is expressed about us when we stumble in either of two ways. As George Buttrick put it, "Heaven laughs, with tears, at our foolish attempts to be more than [human] or less than [human]."[10] We attempt to be more than we are when we attempt the height of angels in one way or another. Perhaps we believe we are wiser, more knowledgeable, or powerful than we are. We may dominate, abuse, enslave, or conquer those whom God loves as much as us. We may forget our days are numbered—that we are dust, frail and temporary, but with God's image within, and God's purposes to serve. When we fall into such "more than ourselves" errors, heaven laughs with tears at us.

There is laughter of derision, also, when we attempt to be less than we are. An example is two men imitating a horse, one the forequarters, the other the hindquarters, with a horse skin thrown over them, perhaps at an ice show. In attempting to take on "horse nature"—at the same time trying to be more than a horse since horses do not skate—they draw the crowd's laughter.

Or, consider a cartoon of a man in a subway, a pigeon on each shoulder. When asked, "Where are you taking them?" he responds, "Don't ask me; they got on at Fifty-ninth Street." The man has become something less—a pigeon perch, even as the pigeons imitate humans in their commute across the city.[11]

There are attempts to be less than we are at which it is harder to laugh. When we give into animal lusts, instincts, impulses, and hungers, we have lost something important. Or when we fall into addictions that dominate our entire attention and energy, or push our own self-interests too hard or abuse others (physically, economically, psychologically, spiritually), we are diminished. God's compassionate / derisive laughter

When I was a student in seminary, one day in theology class, my professor Nels Ferre was exploring the concept of death and its aftermath. He contrasted his view with that of Paul Tillich (with whom he was a friend and friendly competitor) and explained that he believed in a personal conscious life with God, whereas Tillich saw death more as the being of a person returning to the ground of being,—like a raindrop falling into the river. The next day he walked into class chuckling. "Last night, I was thinking," he told us. If Tillich is right, I won't know it. If I am right, Tillich will know it!"

10. Buttrick, "God and Laughter," 55.

11. Both illustrations are from Buttrick, "God and Laughter," 54.

may in turn stir tears and shame in us. Laughter has honesty in it; God's laughter may lead to a facing of ourselves; our sin and our need.

Laughter of Redemption

But that is not the last chapter. There is another kind of divine laughter—loud, hearty, and ringing. It is the laughter of redemption. Lavish, undeserved and unexpected, divine love and grace intervene with God's people time and again. God's laughter in giving is echoed in the delight and joy of those benefiting from these gifts.

God's redeeming actions in *history* call forth the people's praise and celebration.

- In the rescue from bondage in Egypt, "I will sing to the LORD, for he has triumphed gloriously; horse and rider he has thrown into the sea." (Exod 15:1).
- In the deliverance from exile in Babylon, "When the LORD restored the fortunes of Zion, we were like those who dream. Then our mouth was filled with laughter, and our tongue with shouts of joy . . ." (Ps 126:1–2).
- In the life, death, and resurrection of Jesus the Christ, "The sting of death is sin, and the power of the sin is the law. But thanks be to God who gives us the victory through our Lord Jesus Christ." (1 Cor 15:56–57).

God's laughter in redemption touches *individuals* as well.

- Mary, called to be the mother of Jesus, "My soul magnifies the Lord, and my spirit rejoices in God my Savior, for he has looked with favor on the lowliness of his servant . . . ." (Luke 1:47–48a).
- Each of us who wander in one way or another, "Son, you are always with me and all that is mine is yours . . ."
- "But we had to celebrate and rejoice because this brother of yours was dead and has come to life; he was lost and has been found." (Luke 15:31–32).
- Paul, called to Christ's ministry, "Although I am the very least of all the saints, this grace was given to me to bring to the Gentiles the boundless riches of Christ . . . " (Eph 3:8).

- Paul, sustained in difficult times, "What does it matter? Just this, that Christ is proclaimed in every way, whether out of false motives or true and in that I rejoice. Yes, and I will continue to rejoice." (Phil 1:18)

Our redeeming God surprises us time and again, entering into our hopelessness and drawing us out, calling us to participate in the redeeming process, and to hope for the greater glory yet to be. When we recognize this, there is celebration, rejoicing and laughter.

Peter Berger relates the work of the comic to the reality of which we speak. He does so through the concept of transcendence, which he notes is freighted with many meanings. A comic "transcends" the reality of the ordinary by, in some way, offering a different reality, one in which the "assumptions and rules of ordinary life are suspended." This can make life easier to bear, at least temporarily. It is "transcendence in a lower key" without necessarily having any religious implications. However, there is, beyond that, sometimes something in the comic's gift that is not temporary at all. Rather it points to and is an intimation of that vaster world of religious vision.

When we laugh, relax, and enjoy for a few moments, "there is in this transitory experience an intuition, a signal of true redemption, that is, of a world that has been made whole and which the miseries of the human condition have been abolished. This implies transcendence in a higher key; it is religious in the full, proper sense of the word."[12] Such "redeeming laughter," though momentary, is healing in the present, and is both sign and clue of God's greater surprises to come.

We might summarize in this way: First God laughs for us; then God laughs at us; and finally God laughs with us.[13]

THE INTERPLAY OF DIVINE AND HUMAN LAUGHTER

This "redeeming laughter" is seen all the more clearly in three theological concepts that name and identify where God's laughter touches our human experience. Divine and human laughter meet and mingle in joy, in hope, and in grace.

12. Berger, *Redeeeming Laughter*, 205.

13. This is an adaptation of a construct offered in Taylor, "A Theology of Humor," 6.

Joy

An integral part of our relationship with God is joy, which may have many forms of experience and expression. Part of my personal temperament is that I often have a quiet, mostly silent type of joy. People around me may not know how pleased and joyful I am. When, for example, my family is together, I love to sit quietly with them, listen to their stories, and observe them individually and together—young and old. I am soaking up memories that will delight me long after they must go their separate ways.

But, more characteristically, joy's outward expressions include singing, dancing, clapping, playfulness, humor, and laughing. As Conrad Hyers has noted, ". . . though joy and humor are certainly not synonymous, neither are they alien. Humor is not displaced by joy, but is one of its forms of expression."[14] Daniel Migliore (summarizing Barth's view on this topic) states the distinction between humor and joy this way: ". . . humor is different from though intimately related to, joy. Joy arises out of the partial *presence* of the promised Kingdom which has erupted in Christ and in the work of his Spirit. Humor arises out of the still *partial* presence of this kingdom . . . Joy will find its fulfillment in God's new heaven and new earth; humor belongs to a world between the times."[15] Humor, then is small part of the partial and anticipatory joy we can experience in this life and this world.

Further, "joy" and "enjoy" come from the same root and are interrelated in meaning. Thus, enjoyment may be a way we experience part of the joy we are promised. We are drawn to service, caring, worship, study, leadership, in part because that is what we love doing—we enjoy it. Some days may be better than others, but the privilege of being called to tasks that are enriching and fulfilling, that certainly is one aspect of joy.

This blend of joy / humor / enjoyment is a fitting response to the unexpected and incredible goodness of our God. C.S. Lewis said it wonderfully in the title of his autobiography, *Surprised by Joy.* (He originally intended to call his book *Surprised by a Sudden Manifestation of the Christophanic Theophany,* but a wise editor talked him out of it.[16] They got it right!) Frederick Buechner elaborates—"Happiness turns up more

14. Hyers, *Holy Laughter*, 239.

15. Migliore, "Reappraising Barth's Theology," 239.

16. Darden, *Jesus Laughed*, 119.

or less where you'd expect it to—a good marriage, a rewarding job, a pleasant vacation. Joy, on the other hand, is as notoriously unpredictable as the one who bequeaths it."[17]

If indeed, joy is the most unmistakable sign of the presence of God, this joy is not only a spontaneous happening from time to time. It is also a posture, an attitude, a belief, an expectancy to be cultivated. Spontaneous laughter may be an expression of—and an invitation to—joy. But a systematic practice of playfulness, trust, and resulting smiles and laughter may stir this gift of joy when it is missing or release it when it needs expression.

Our spiritual concept of joy reminds us that such times of mirth and gladness are "God things." Humor is often laughter within the joy of the Christian faith. It is a gay laughter of belief in an ultimate ground of being that touches us in a healing and vitalizing way.

Hope

Humor is also connected to Christian hope. What is hope? It is the conviction that the present problems and dilemmas are not the last word. It is anticipation that divine forces are at work that can and will alter the course of affairs. William Barclay said it well, "The Christian hope is not simply a trembling, hesitant hope that perhaps the promises of God may be true. It is the confident expectation that they cannot be anything else than true."[18]

A reflection from Sue Monk Kidd is instructive here. She wrote about a time of struggle and pain during a spiritual transition in her life.

"I remembered that when Ann [her daughter] was four, she tugged on my skirt for attention and asked, 'Mama, does God laugh?' God *laugh?* The idea had never entered my head. (I suppose that's one reason we have children, to make us think of inexplicable things.) 'Why do you ask?' I said to her.

"'Because I think I heard him today,' she said.

"I gathered her into my arms. 'Yes, of course God laughs,' I whispered. Maybe that's what life is, I thought: God laughing, God rejoicing.

17. Buechner, *Wishful Thinking*, 47.

18. Barclay, *More New Testament Words*, 46.

"Eckhart wrote that God laughed into our soul, bringing us joy. He also believed that God suffered. I had no problem with his suffering . . . Perhaps, like Ann, I needed to listen to God laughing."[19]

ACTUAL CHILDREN'S LETTERS TO GOD COLLECTED BY A MINISTER IN MONTANA

Dear God, In school they told us what you do. Who does it when You are on vacation? —Jane

Dear God, I went to this wedding and they kissed right in church. Is that ok? —Neil

Dear God, Did You really mean "do unto others as they do unto you"? Because if You did, then I'm going to fix my brother! —Darla

Dear God, Thank you for the baby brother, but what I prayed for was a puppy. —Joyce

Dear God, Please send me a pony. I never asked for anything before, You can look it up. —Bruce

Dear God, I bet it is very hard for You to love all of everybody in the whole world. There are only 4 people in our family and I can never do it. —Nan

Dear God, We read Thomas Edison made light. But in school they said You did it. So I bet he stoled your idea. Sincerely, —Donna. (from a circulated email.)

And what is that link between humor and hope? The guffaw or chuckle in a seemingly hopeless situation is a hint that the laugher doesn't quite believe it is hopeless. In such a circumstance, rather, laughter is expressing what of what Viktor Frankl called "the last human freedom," the freedom to pick one's attitude, perspective, and expectation.[20]

Humor and laughter, then, are at both ends of the hope process. A smile or chuckle may be an invitation to hope, its first expression. And then, after hope is more firmly embraced, it may issue in a more confident laughter.

19. Kidd, *When the Heart Waits*, 98–99.

20. Frankl, *Man's Search for Meaning*, 104.

Grace

In speaking of joy and hope, we have already spoken of grace. Grace is God's unmerited, unconditional love that creates, restores, forgives, and grants newness of life to individuals, community, and world. Grace is God calling ordinary human beings into faith, into community, into service and leadership. Grace is the lightness and happiness we feel when we have been forgiven and called. Grace is life in living color. Grace is a cold drink on a hot day, a person to love, a child to cherish. In the words of the Psalmist, grace is "the goodness of the Lord in the land of the living."(Ps 27:13) And it is more.

The grace of which I speak is both a constant in God's relationship with us and a fresh event that is experienced time and again. With each new experience—treasured in itself and as reminder of God's steadfast love—we sing and celebrate and give thanks. Laughter is fitting and often present.

This leads me to believe that humor is an integral part of apprehending and embracing the whole Christian proclamation. God's laughter is seen in creating us, in responding to our failings, and in redeeming us. God's humor intermingles with our own in many ways, at very least in joy, hope, and grace.

For those of us who are Christian leaders, this perspective offers both resource and responsibility. We are offered enhanced possibilities for proclaiming and living the gospel. At the same time we are called to exercise this in a way that is fitting with the theology we have just articulated. Part of this is to believe in it, claim it for ourselves, practice it consistently, and feel its buoyancy holding us up when other circumstances would pull us down. Another part is to use it in a fitting manner with those we lead and serve. (We'll talk about this aspect—using humor in ministry and service—in the next three chapters.)

A GRATEFUL AND RESPONSIBLE STEWARDSHIP

We have occasion for profound gratitude—for this life of joy, hope, grace. But every gift from God is to be managed responsibly and accountably, lest it become calloused and lest it be abused. An ethic and etiquette of the spiritual practice of humor and play is needed. We now attempt to formulate that ethic.

Peter Berger guides us into exploring our ethical response when he notes that "humorlessness is a cognitive handicap." Inability in humor may render a person incapable of certain insights, ways of seeing things, perhaps entire spheres of reality. We have been contending that humor awakens one to the vitality and beauty of the Christian proclamation.

Then Berger goes on to ask, "Could it [i.e., humorlessness] also be a moral fault?"[21] He is hard put for an answer, as are we. On the one hand, there is much about humor that is an aid to ethics and being moral. Relaxation, lessening of tension, "aha" moments of a wider perspective, insight into another's point of view may all come with humor and laughter.

On the other hand, we must acknowledge that humor can be used for morally reprehensible purposes as well. Laughter at an individual may pressure one into conformity. Wit can be exercised with malice or hurt as an intention. A person attempting to be funny can be insensitive to another's pain or one may unconsciously lapse into sarcasm or cynicism and inflict pain on self and other.

Further, humor can become an avoidance device. One can escape into humor to avoid hard intellectual labor, moral accountability, or religious commitment. One can choose simply to laugh and ignore rather than wrestle with the hard and tragic questions confronting humankind. Or, humor may be used to divert and avoid a conflict that is better faced and resolved. If humorlessness is a moral blindness problem of some of us, probably more of us are guilty at times of insensitivity or wrong use of the humor we possess.

The practice of humor is one of God's fragile gifts,

EPITAPHS WITH A TWIST

Have mercy on my soul, Lord God
As I on you, were I Lord God
And you were Martin Elginbrod.

Who far below this tomb dost rest,
Has joined the army of the blest.
The Lord has taken her to the sky,
The saints rejoice and so do I.

Under this sod and under these trees
Lieth the body of Solomon Pease.
He's not in this hole,
But only his pod;
He shelled out his soul
And went up to God.

(Capps, *Laughter*. He took these from Tibballs, *The Mammoth Book of Jokes*, 367–384.)

21. Berger, 152–153.

a gift that can both be lost and exploited. As with God's other gifts, it requires a thoughtful and reverent stewardship. This stewardship is so that it might fulfill God's purposes in trusting us with it.

The setting of koinonia / community

We are called into a community. In this community we are fellow workers, participants, servants of one another. And, the New Testament gives this community lofty names—family of God, even "Body of Christ."

Ordinary human beings, no better and no worse than others are called into this fellowship (the Greek term for it is *koinonia*). We humans, coming into God's grace will have the usual range of human problems with each other. This will include competition, gossip, envy, conflict, among others. Though all too common, they can destroy or hurt this *koinonia* into which we are called.

In the New Testament, much guidance is given for our life together. This provides us with the setting for our ethic of humor. Two Bible passages on this theme are particularly instructive. In his letter to the Philippians, after a gentle call to resolve some differences, Paul calls upon this church to follow some qualities well-known and admired in their culture, "Finally, beloved, whatever is true, whatever is honorable, whatever is just, whatever is pure, whatever is pleasing, whatever is commendable, if there is any excellence and if there is anything worthy of praise, think about these things." (Phil 4:8). That provides a starting place in our ethic of humor.

Further, in his letter to Galatians, Paul lists many "works of the flesh" including some that directly destroy community, "enmities, strife, jealousy, anger, quarrels, dissensions, factions, envy." Then he goes on, "By contrast, the fruit of the Spirit is love, joy, peace, patience, kindness, generosity, faithfulness, gentleness, and self-control." (Gal 5:20–22). Combined, these passages say to live the finest values of your culture, and seek God's spiritual fruits to be able to do so.

While humor is not specifically mentioned, there is strong and helpful guidance here. This *koinonia* is a trust from God, precious in God's sight, though frail and vulnerable. Do all you can to sustain and nourish it: avoid that which will destroy or damage it.

We are also called to affirm the finest values of our culture. There are some contemporary comics who assault sexual morality and other sensitive human relations as well. Humor should be challenged to elevate, not degrade individual and community courtesy and behavioral norms.

At its best, one of humor's gifts is that it can contribute to intimacy. We can see the humanity of the other, and recognize our own shortcomings. That is certainly one of the possibilities to be cultivated and practiced.

The purpose of humor—healing and 1oining in God's redemption

Further, we are to consider the purpose of one's speech and conversation. In Ephesians we read, "Let no evil talk come out of your mouths, but only what is useful for building up, as there is need, so that your words may give grace to those who hear." (Eph 4:29).

If grace is a sign of God's goodness in our lives, then speech, including humor should build up and impart grace. Benign humor, including laughter at self can do that. So can tragicomedy, humor as consolation in the midst of tragedy. Humor may encourage self care. It may help one keep a sense of balance and help reframe issues and problems in a different light.

Humor can do those things, but it is by no means automatic. Humor that might have been fun and helpful with one person or group in one situation may be inappropriate and harmful in another.

And so a fair question is "What is my intention with this humor?" Not only does the professional comedian need a sense of timing, so does the Christian leader / caregiver. A series of considerations is in order. Where—in what setting—is this humor to be used? When—at what point in our journey or in our relationship—will I venture humor? Why—is it simply my way with people, or is there specific hope and objective—am I using this humor?

Granted, that's a lot to think about with something that often just happens spontaneously. Still, I submit, these are valuable questions to consider in prospect and retrospect, to increase the appropriateness of humor in ministry. We are speaking not only of ethics, but of etiquette, the considerate and respectful care of people.

Satire, irony, parody?

So far we have been speaking of a humor ethic for those within the loving community and in relationships that are hopefully redemptive. But much of the world and, sadly, much of the church do not fit that description. There is injustice, unequal power, institutional cruelty, and strongly / violently differing opinions on many crucial topics.

As we have noted over and again, for a long time, satire and parody of an opponent has been a weapon in such conflicts. It has been one method available to the less powerful in such struggles. Is this to be allowed or disallowed in an ethic of humor?

Clearly, as we are attentive to the biblical witness, this type of humor cannot be entirely disallowed. For example, in Jeremiah's call, he is appointed, "to pluck up and pull down, to destroy and overthrow, to build and to plant." (Jer 1:10). Both the assault on people's pretensions and false powers—by whatever means—and the building up of a people with a new covenant were parts of his mission.

As we further explore scripture, we find satire and parody again and again. Foreign conquering powers and their arrogant leaders as well as idols and false worship are disdainfully described. Corrupt religious and political leaders of their own people as well as people's spiritual laziness come under prophetic attack and rebuke. Jesus' speech of woes on Scribes and Pharisees (Matt 23: 13–36) was satire that was strong, probing, and poignant.

Out of the biblical witness, we conclude there are times when satire is appropriate and necessary. We must next ask—then and now—when are those times and what are the conditions? I suggest these guidelines:

a. Satire should be used only after all other attempts at communication, persuasion, resolution, and reconciliation have failed.

b. It is more permissible for those without power and with no other means, something of a last resort.

c. Even then, the question needs to be asked of fairness and accuracy of the satire or parody.

d. The "weapon" of humor should fit the conflict. Earlier we distinguished between satire (which aims at debunking and destroying) and irony (which is a more loving look at human foibles and failings). Is one more fitting than the other?

e. Further, there needs to be cautious awareness of a related attitude. I speak of cynicism which arises out of depression and despair and may become a habit of debunking of anything that disappoints. This danger merits thoughtful self attention and possible change of attitude and method.

Puritanism in modern dress?

It might be objected that I ask too much. This guidance might feel like a new form of the old Puritanism. Thinking of all these things can interfere with one's timing of humor and reduce one's spontaneity. The result could be that a book on humor as a spiritual practice diminishes its use!

My ethical discussion may have that impact, at least temporarily. The purpose of this book is to work in two directions—to broaden understanding of the variety of types and benefits from humor practices, but also to encourage thoughtful examination and abandoning of unhelpful humor practices. Hopefully, the reader will be stretched both ways.

But, one might further ask, what about the "naughty pleasures" of humor? What about those nights when good friends gather, enjoy each other, and joke / laugh about such topics as sex, the battle between the genders, the races, religions, and such? I am not one to judge what occurs in such happenings between confidential good friends. Certainly I could not be the one to cast the first stone. If this happens may it be the occasional exception, not the rule.

At the same time, I do advocate humor as a spiritual practice of ministry and caring. The goal is a constant, wise and fitting, broad-ranging humor that is life-building, sustaining, renewing, and uplifting for church leader, congregation, and world.

QUESTIONS FOR PERSONAL AND GROUP REFLECTION

1. What metaphors / images for God are at the heart of your theology?
2. How does the image of "laughing God" strike you? How important or central should it be, in your opinion? How does it influence other aspects of your theology?
3. Reflect on the threefold schema: God's laughter of creation; God's laughter of derision; God's laughter of redemption. In what ways is this faithful Christian theology? In what ways does it need to be challenged, expanded, or otherwise modified?

4. What are your thoughts on the interaction of humor and joy, humor and hope, humor and grace? Where did you agree with what the chapter suggested? Where disagree? What would you add?
5. What strikes you as helpful in my suggestions about an ethic and etiquette of humor? What doesn't? What would you add or change?
6. What are you learning about humor as a spiritual practice for you personally?

6

Laughter in the Crying Places

(Humor and the Caregiver)

In a cartoon strip, an AIDS patient when asked, "How can you joke at a time like this?" responds, "How can you not?"[1]

We will likely spend much time among persons with big or persisting problems, harsh pains, or unrelenting grief. This may be a one-time encounter or a long term relationship.

In all this, we offer people some very simple things—our presence, listening, a caring smile, and words (including prayers)—either our own or something we read to them. We believe,—indeed we have been told—that these simple acts are appreciated, welcome, sometimes even healing and transforming.

Is there any place for humor when we extend care in this arena of human suffering, finitude, and grieving? I say yes, both for us and the persons for whom we care. As for us, it is important that we recognize what a privilege it is to be close to people in these deep places of their lives. This sense of grace and privilege may kindle joy in us as caregivers. When our practice of joy / wonder / humor shows in our presence / listening / words, good things happen. Again, this is not only for us but for the other as well.

I believe this, and in this chapter I will tell you why. I will take you on a quick journey through pastoral care situations in general, then pre-marriage preparation, grief ministries, and more intensive pastoral counseling. In each of these ministry situations, we will consider humor opportunities, practices, options, and benefits. I will tell you about my

1. Klein, *The Courage to Laugh*, 40.

experiences and reflections, what other pastors and caregivers have told me, and what some insightful authors think.

PASTORAL CARE IN GENERAL

I remember two pre-surgery calls when there was no question about humor. The patients provided it in abundance. The first was with a man, a middle school guidance counselor, known for his love of life and his playful teasing ways. In his pre-op nervousness, these qualities were coming through in abundance. Every little statement or pre-op procedure stirred yet another quip or comeback from him. The patient, nurses, family, and minister were all laughing uproariously. This continued until he was wheeled into his surgical procedure.

The second time was with a young man, son of the first, an aspiring actor, in for some cosmetic surgery. Equally playful, he had his family bring their video camera. Each visitor or hospital staff person was subjected to a brief on-camera interview, all to great hilarity.

I thoroughly enjoyed myself and laughed much both times. At the same time, I am confident they appreciated my being there as friend / pastor, as a calm presence and as representative of their church and faith. After the laughter there was the much more subdued waiting during the surgery. Happily, both surgery patients came through fine.

But what about times when it is not as clear? The ministers I consulted had varied responses. Beverly Lowell noted, "I do a lot of in-home visits, and I try to be light hearted and find humor in small things to ease the initial time. But I drop it once we get into the heart of the visit." Other ministers commented "only when appropriate," and that is certainly wise advice that assumes the health and sensitivity of the caregiver. We are speaking of a wide range of experiences from white hot crises to chronic and debilitating diseases that may go on for years. Our approach must vary with each person's temperament and circumstance. But what is appropriate when, and how do we know? We will consider those questions in this chapter.

Insights from other caring professions

Raymond Moody, M.D., in his fascinating book, *Laugh after Laugh: the Healing Power of Humor,* points to a fascinating use of humor in healing that has been little noticed. That is the uncanny ability of the clown to break through to persons who may be severely withdrawn and unresponsive. He tells of a clown whose face is known to many walking through a large hospital when he saw a little girl with a doll of his likeness. The girl was being fed by a nurse. "As the clown walked in, the child said his name, whereupon the nurse threw down the spoon and dashed off to call the physician. For the child, diagnosed as catatonic, had been unresponsive for six months. The doctor was able to get her to follow up this first communication and the child progressively improved . . ."[2]

Another example—a 95-year-old-man was admitted to a hospital, severely depressed. He had neither eaten nor spoken a word to anyone for days. Medical staff were alarmed and believed he would soon die. "A clown entered his hospital room and within thirty minutes had succeeded in getting the elderly man to talk, to laugh, and to eat. The man lived for several more years and the clown maintained communication with him during this time."[3] This is not at all surprising, particularly in the light of the fact that a number of sources, from varying times in church history, have portrayed Christ as a clown.[4]

For yet another perspective, Allen Klein experienced the power of humor through the heartbreak of his wife's illness and death from a rare liver disease. He recalled that she wanted the male nude foldout from a *Playgirl* magazine taped on the wall of her hospital room. When he feared it too risqué, they put it up anyway, but placed a leaf from a plant over the sensitive part. Day by day as the leaf shriveled—and her disease progressed—they laughed at the leaf. Out of memory and tribute to this valiantly humorous woman and this discovery, he developed a new career of doing speeches and seminars on the value of humor in such dire settings, calling himself *a jollyologist.* He also wrote books that contain powerful testimony and example of the power of humor in the illnesses, mishaps, and tragedies of life.[5] I heartily commend them to you.

Many others affirmed the value and power of humor in the pain and tragedy of life. Erma Bombeck noted, "Laughter rises out of tragedy when you need it the most and rewards you for your courage." Peter Weingold, M.D., adds, "Finding humor in a tragic situation is an ex-

2. Moody, *Laugh After Laugh*, 21.

3. Ibid.

4. Feaster, "The Importance of Humor and Clowning," 380–87.

5. Of Allen Klein's many books, three of particular interest are *The Courage to Laugh, The Healing Power of Humor*, and *Learning to Laugh When You Feel Like Crying.*

tremely healthy step. It is a way of looking forward to the future and of saying that this suffering can be put behind us . . . It is a way of saying, 'This tragedy has *happened* to us, but it does not *define* us. Despite what we've been through, we are going ahead with our lives . . . You didn't destroy us! We are still here. We are still laughing. And therefore we have life and hope.'"[6]

Consider the experience of Oliver Sacks, well-known author and neurologist. Sacks was hiking on a desolate mountaintop in Norway when he was attacked by a bull that rendered him helpless. He thought he would perish, but then two people found him. In his "broken Norwegian" he tried to explain what had happened and supplement it with drawing in the dust.

Sacks continues, "The two of them [his rescuers] laughed at my picture of the bull. They were full of humor, these two, and as they laughed I laughed too—and suddenly with the laughter, the tragic tension exploded, and I felt vividly and, so to speak, comically alive once again . . . [I]t now occurred to me—I hadn't laughed once. Now I couldn't stop laughing—the laughter of relief, and the laughter of love, that deep-down laughter which comes from the center of one's being. The silence was exploded, that quiet quite deathly silence which had seized me, as in a spell, those last minutes."[7]

Klein also told a story about a colleague, Steve Wilson, who presents humor programs as he does. Steve was asked to speak at a cancer clinic to a support group called "Make Today Count." Since Steve's mother had died of ovarian cancer, he thought it would be great if he could be helpful to these people.

As the group of about thirty people gathered, each introduced oneself by name, kind of cancer, and stage of treatment. It hit Steve how grave the situation of almost everyone in the room, and he found himself feeling inadequate and uncertain whether it was right to discuss humor in such circumstances.

And so he offered a little prayer, asking God that if this is where God wanted him to be, to guide him in sharing what would truly helpful. This is prayer had a twofold answer. The first was when a man introduced himself, "My name is Lester and I'm pissed off. I have cancer of the liver.

6. Both quotes are from Klein, *The Courage to Laugh*, 3, 14.

7. Ibid., 25–26. He is quoting Sacks, *A Leg to Stand On*.

My doctor told me I had six months to live. That was a year ago—and I gave away my winter coat."

When everyone laughed, Steve felt validation. He went into his presentation, telling jokes, playing with props, exploring the contributions of humor. People were having a good time, appreciative, and responding with much laughter

Then there was a knock on the door. A woman came in and said, "Listen, I'm trying to run a support group in the next room." He thought he was in trouble for being too boisterous, but the woman went on, "[M]y group would like to come in and join your group." That group was a grief recovery group for those who had recently lost a loved one.

That was the second answer to Wilson's prayer. He concluded, "People who came to support each other in their grief wanted to be where the laughter was."[8]

Furthermore, humor has even been found to be helpful for those whose situation is terminal. Kay Ann Herth did research, interviewing fourteen patients with a prognosis of six months or less to live. When asked about humor, eighty-five percent of them thought humor would be helpful, but only fourteen percent experienced the presence of any humor.

Dr. Herth heard such comments as "I try to be playful, but others won't respond." "If I ever needed humor it is now." "I want to smile and laugh, but that upsets my family."

She noted a number of contributions of humor for these terminal patients:

- *Humor helped a patient's self-esteem*—participants felt like "a real person again" because they were sharing something positive.
- *Humor altered a patient's attitude*—it enabled them to see things more positively and helped them "put a new light on their situation."
- *Humor aided a patient's communication*—it "allowed them to ask questions that they might otherwise not ask and to hear instructions they might otherwise be too anxious to hear."[9]

8. Ibid., 198–99. The story is summarized. The parts in quotation marks are direct quotes.

9. Ibid., 71. The patients' comments and the list are direct quotes.

Specific pastoral opportunities

So then, how does the pastoral caregiver relate to the humor potential in caring for the suffering? Should a rubber nose and grease paint be packed in the minister's kit along with a Bible and prayer book? Not necessarily, certainly not for those who would find that out of character. Still, there are possibilities.

To begin, at very least we can be sensitive and responsive to the often subtle and hidden humor expressed by the person being visited.

- A person long confined to a wheel chair greeted me with, "I'd love to get up and make you a cup of tea."
- In her final weeks, my mom hated the hospital food served to her and the scolding nurses aides gave her for not eating. In between times, she enjoyed telling exaggerated stories about how bad it was.
- Margaret, an elderly member no longer able to drive, would call for a taxi any Sunday morning she felt well enough to go to church, knowing someone would take her home afterward. One Sunday, all that was available was a huge limousine. She was delighted, hoped there would be people outside at church to see her arrival, and called to tell me about

Aging People Laughing at Themselves

I feel like my body has gotten totally out of shape, so I got my doctor's permission to join a fitness club and start exercising. I decided to take an aerobics class for seniors. I bent, twisted, gyrated, jumped up and down, and perspired for an hour. But, by the time I got my leotards on, the class was over.

An elderly woman decided to prepare her will and told her preacher she had two final requests. First, she wanted to be cremated, and second, she wanted her ashes scattered over Walmart. "Walmart?" the preacher exclaimed. "Why Walmart?" "Then I'll be sure my daughters visit me twice a week!"

My memory's not as sharp as it used to be. Also, my memory's not as sharp as it used to be.

The Senility Prayer: Grant me the senility to forget the people I never liked anyway, the good fortune to run into the ones I do, and the eyesight to tell the difference." (Excerpt, circulated email)

it that afternoon. She liked it that I told others who kidded her about her regal ride. Margaret asked the limousine driver's name and would call the taxi company and request him and his elegant vehicle from time to time.

Such gentle expressions of courageous self-humor deserve recognition, encouragement, and mutual enjoyment. We can at least do that. But there is more.

We can be aware that there might be humor lurking within the situation and inquire about it. This may be particularly so if we have known the person to have enjoyed humor before but seem to be lacking it now. Along with our other questions of concern, we can ask such things as, "Have you laughed since you have been here? Is there anything about this that makes you feel like laughing? Have you ever been through anything like this and laughed about it later?"

I recently was reminded of a caution about humor in pastoral care. I called on a good clergy friend following hernia surgery. We started with our usual teasing. But he suddenly stopped and said sharply. "Don't make me laugh. It hurts my incision." The caution I should have remembered—on surgery wards, go gently. Be aware of what surgery has happened and the impact laughing may have on one's body and comfort.

Two-way ministry

And, though we do not go asking to be ministered to, we can also allow the courage and laughter of those we visit care for us. For those of us who minister with eyes to see and ears to hear, this happens again and again. I smile, recalling the playful excitement of a frail 85-year-old woman when told there had been a "cute" 85-year-old man admitted to the same ward. With a twinkle in her eyes, she told me of her ideas how to get in to meet him.

I remember Shawn, age nine, terminally ill with a rare form of cancer. He always had jokes, riddles, or favorite pages from comics to show me when I called. Patient and pastor ministered to each other.

This was also the insight gained by some of the persons reported in Klein's books. One of them, Donna Strickland recalls that at the end of a long, exhausting day, she was asked by a nurse on the hospice unit to make one more visit, this one to a dying man who needed to talk about death.

She went in and was flustered to see an extremely gaunt man, all flesh and bones, and she began clumsily. She recalls, "He looked up at me with the bluest, brightest eyes I had ever seen. He said, 'Looks like you have had a pretty rough day.' Since she had mentioned she came to talk about death, he went on, "It was last week I was concerned about death. I'm not anymore. Hey, why not sit down and let me tell you my favorite joke."

As tears streamed down Donna's face, he asked, "'What has 75 balls and drives old ladies crazy?' 'Oh, Good Lord, what?' 'Bingo!'"

She concludes, "We laughed as if it were the best and finest joke either of us had ever heard—and we cried as if there were no tomorrow. I left his room knowing I had been given a rare gift of a lifetime."[10]

There is yet another thing to be said about pastoral care. We pastoral caregivers go embodying a laughing, loving God expressed in our believing joy, hope, and grace. As we read in Romans, ". . . we rejoice in our sufferings, knowing that suffering produces endurance, and endurance produces character, and character produces hope, and hope does not disappoint us, because God's love has been poured into our hearts . . ." (Rom 5:3–5a, RSV). As those who are there to represent hope and joy and grace, always sensitively, we should be ready to invite the humor and laughter that our Christian faith implies.

We now turn to two specific areas of pastoral care.

PRE-MARRIAGE PREPARATION

A wedding is a public event where many components all come together. There are at least these: (a) a culmination of romance and friendship; (b) religious beliefs, heritage, and rituals; (c) legal contract and obligations; (d) a major family transition; (e) a party-celebration with friends and family; and (f) cultural assumptions and impact.

Beyond that, the couple who comes to the minister to be married may have a wide range of issues and concerns of their own. They may be in an early stage of the deep relationship that sustains marriage, may be in denial about their problems, and may be avoiding conflicts (perhaps not knowing how to deal with them). They may have idealistic images of their own bond and of the wedding they envision. And, they may be nervous about talking with a minister, afraid s/he might ask too many personal questions. This is a time of searching, exploration, and testing

10. Ibid., He is quoting Wooten, *Heart, Humor, and Healing.*

(not all engagements end in marriages!),—and possibly denial that such is needed. A few couples may be making a mistake and may discover so in the pre-marriage conversations.

As a couple and their families of origin move toward a wedding, there will likely be conflict. Many families have at least one "melt down" during the pre-wedding tensions.

How should a minister approach this opportunity of helping a couple / family prepare for the marriage and the wedding? A calm perspective on all the components competing for attention will help keep the minister, and in turn the couple and their families, mostly centered and usually on course.

> A woman called and made an appointment with a counselor. When she arrived, she said she wanted to talk about her marriage. Though the counselor usually only talked with couples, he decided to get an idea of their situation. He asked, "Do you have a grudge?" She responded, "No, but we have a nice carport." The counselor next asked, "Do you have grounds?" "Oh yes," she responded, "more than an acre, and we grow most of our own vegetables."
>
> The counselor asked, "Does he beat you up?" "Oh no," she answered. "I usually get up and make coffee and breakfast while he gets ready to go to work." Frustrated, the counselor asked, "Why are you here?" "It's that husband of mine," she responded. "He just can't communicate!"

A gracious, hospitable welcome is a good start. I used to cover the door to my office with cartoons, poking gentle fun at ministers, counselors, and churches. Not only counselees, but many others visited my door to see what was new there. Bob Overstreet notes, "My concern is that the pastor needs to be pleasant, friendly, and gracious in these settings, instead of pompous, arrogant and egotistical. A sense of humor can make all the difference, but it can't be forced nor be artificial. We need just to help people smile and relax, and it can happen when we set the example."

Such a mood can enhance the continued conversation. Heather Entrekin uses a conversation "game" with couples in which they compare responses to statements about marriage. For a series of questions they discuss—does each partner agree, disagree, or find oneself not sure? She reflects, "They produce much laughter" [and, I am sure, the decrease of defense and denial]. So I shall keep using them."

This perspective can continue through rehearsal and other preparations. A wedding rehearsal can begin with affirmation that our God of love created us for each other and rejoices with us in this couple's love, commitment, and beginning of the marriage journey. There is room for playfulness in working through the details of a rehearsal. We will speak of the wedding ceremony in the next chapter.

A minister needs to maintain that practice of humor about all the various elements converging and competing in a wedding. I recall a time when the mother of a bride came up to me after a wedding and gushed, "Wasn't that a beautiful wedding?" She turned and walked off, and then said over her shoulder, "Oh, and your part was ok, too."

This was after months of sessions with her daughter and fiancé in which they had carefully worked with me in pre-marriage counseling and in creating a thoughtful, faithful wedding service. This included the creation / adaptation of vows that expressed beautifully their shared covenant. *I* thought that was the best part, but, oh well.

And this mother was a faithful church person. When we extend wedding services to the lightly or un-churched, the confusion may grow even more. It's good to relax and keep smiling.

BEREAVEMENT, GRIEVING, FUNERALS

A frequent claim on our pastoral care is the death of a person and the grieving, ministry, and services that are needed.

Kenneth Mitchell and Herbert Anderson have succinctly and accurately noted – "Grief is the normal but bewildering cluster of ordinary human emotions arising in response to a significant loss, intensified and complicated by the relationship to the person or the object lost. Guilt, shame, loneliness, anxiety, anger, terror, bewilderment, emptiness, profound sadness, despair, helplessness are all part of grief and all are common to being human. Grief is the clustering of some or all of these emotions in response to loss"[11]

Further, there are specific tasks of "grief work" in a grief process that will persist for months and years if the grieving person is to grow and heal.

11. Mitchell and Anderson, *All Our Losses, All Our Griefs*, 54–55.

Gentle healing humor?

Is there any room for humor in all this? Among this "cluster of emotions" is it possible there is relief, gratitude, remembrance? Should there be clergy use of humor? Some say no. In American society, denial of death, and the rushing and trivialization of grief is far too common. We should not be part of anything that diverts people from the necessary grieving process.

On the other hand, there may be times when humor may enhance one's grieving process and help name the hope that sustains. Or laughter may provide a brief, needed respite from the deep pain of grief. I remember when my father died (I was not quite ten years old), a church family called on us. Their son, a couple years older than I, went down to my room with me, and he took out one of my games. We played, I became engrossed, and at one point I laughed out loud. I still remember my surprise at the sound of my own laughter. It contained a hint that I might laugh again some day, something I could not imagine before that during those terrible times.

At the time of a death, many of us pastors sit down with as much of the family as possible. In addition to making plans for the funeral, we invite memory sharing and storytelling about the person who died. Sometimes with very little urging, treasured stories that include smiles and laughter begin to flow. This contributes to a healing grieving process. With permission, some of these stories may be recalled at the funeral. I am convinced that memories are a gift that God gives us so that we have something of a loved one after that person dies. As pastor, I am wise to invite the sharing of memories, not running away from the hurt, anger, or laughter and humor that may be in those stories. There have been times when grieving families have thanked me for the service, but even more for sitting down and listening to their family stories, laughing and crying with them. One person told me, "That was our real memorial service, wasn't it?"

John Blythe recalls an occasion when grief and humor came together naturally. A member of his congregation, Charles Trent, was a retired minister. Charles was a self-taught handyman and a great friend of the Southeast Asian refugees moving into their community. Charles would help them fix up their homes, but in his own way and not usually according to local building codes. There was a time when a frustrated city inspector, looking at some of this improvised work, asked John, "How do you put a retired minister in jail?"

One day Charles was cutting down a tree in one of these new residents' yard and suddenly died of a heart attack. At Charles' funeral, John told of the inspector's question. It so aptly described that generous, free spirited man, the congregation roared with laughter.

At the same time, we clergy are often the butt of jokes about funeral sermons that described the deceased so glowingly that no one recognizes the person. There needs to be integrity in what we say. Humor should be used only when it is accurately and fittingly called forth by memories and grieving friends and family.

We caregivers are also wise to remember that the grieving goes on long after the funeral or memorial service. Sensitive caring people need to be available to persons in that continued grieving. It may be that only when some of the grieving has had its course that the humorous times can be recalled and cherished. The three friends I mention in chapter one have all been dead for a number of years. I still miss them, but increasingly I am upheld by the laughter we shared. We enjoyed each other and celebrated our friendship when they were alive. I now chuckle at those memories and am comforted, grateful that they were part of my life.

PASTORAL COUNSELING

In addition to offering pastoral care, ministers and other caregivers sometimes do pastoral counseling, a more structured, contracted arrangement for a series of focused conversations. For many, this is short term, single issue, solution-based counseling that is appropriate for one with basic training in ministry. For others with more training, it may also involve deeper, multi-faceted, long term sessions where more specialized or complex needs can be addressed. Either type can be with an individual or a couple or family. All we have said up to now in this chapter applies here. Are there any additions?

A list of possibilities

Waleed Anthony Salameh describes twelve therapeutic humor techniques. These may also possibly be useful in pastoral counseling. Here are the techniques mentioned.

1. Surprise—the using of unexpected occurrences, such as a drilling noise outside to communicate a therapeutic message, or to respond in a totally unexpected way.
2. Exaggeration—the playful use of clear and obvious over- or understatement.
3. Absurdity—bringing in something that is "foolish, nonsensical, inane, disordered . . . without having any logical reason to be."
4. The human condition—speaking of problems most humans encounter in a humorous manner to emphasize their commonality.
5. Incongruity—bringing together two or more "usually incompatible ideas, feelings, situations, objects, etc."
6. Confrontation / affirmation humor—confronting a person's maladaptive or self-defeating behaviors while at the same time expressing care and affirmation of the patient as a person.
7. Word play—"using puns, double entendres, witticisms, song lines, and well known quotes or sayings from popular culture to convey therapeutic messages."
8. Metaphorical mirth—"using metaphorical constructions, analogies, fairy tales, and allegories for therapeutic story telling."
9. Impersonation—imitating or copying typical statements or other maladaptive styles of the patient or those spoken of in the counseling.
10. Relativizing—putting things within a larger context so that they lose their absolute power or meaning.
11. The tragic-comic twist—a very delicate strategy that attempts to turn a "patient's detrimental tragic energies into constructive comical energies."
12. Bodily humor—using the body or parts of it, perhaps imitating the patient's mannerisms to convey messages and suggestions to the patient.[12]

That provides a broad brush overview of some of the possibilities. For most of us, some of these would be more natural and comfortable than others. I myself am most likely to use "the human condition" to

12. Capps, *A Time to Laugh*, 142–43. He is summarizing information from Salameh, "Humor in Psychotherapy," 61–88.

put a problem in perspective; "incongruity" to help a person see self-contradictions;' "confrontation / affirmation" hoping that loving, caring plus confrontation will equal change. I might slip in wordplays and various story / metaphors when the opportunity arose. Some of the rest do not fit my rather gentle "I am here and have time for you" style.

Possible additions to the list

This list also misses a couple vital opportunities. One is the self-humor of which we have spoken. I recall especially one pastor friend. When the newspapers started telling of people suing ministers for malpractice, he wrote telling his congregation not to bother suing him for malpractice. He went on that he was human and fallible, and they all knew that very well. If they wanted his care and counsel, he would gladly provide it. But they needed to know that they were the ones who finally had to decide and choose. The combination (and incongruity) of pastor / counselor authority and humility provides opportunity for humor.

Another humor opportunity may arise in the conflict between what the client wants and needs. With some of my counselees and students, I desire their autonomy and self-direction, and they want me to tell them what to do. When that conflict emerges, they hear my mildly funny, but consistent line, "Advice and a couple dollars will get you a cup of coffee."

> Two women met at a party after having not seen each other for years. After they greeted each other, the first woman noted her friend was wearing an extraordinary diamond and commented, "That is the most beautiful and enormous diamond I have ever seen." Her friend responded, "Yes, it is an unusual diamond. It is the Calahan Diamond. And it comes complete with the Calahan curse." The first woman wanted to know, "What is the Calahan curse?" She responded, "Mr. Calahan." (Told by Bruce Larson, *There's a Lot More to Health Than Not Being Sick*, 41–42.)

Humor occasions

This list also calls to mind several thoughts—not so much about humor techniques, but about occasions for humor within pastoral counseling, mine and others'.

One of my counseling supervisors used to tell me, "Counseling is where you go to be held accountable for your bulls_ _ _." Accountability, honesty, facing what a person had ignored or missed—that is a great gift of counseling. Sometimes humor helps this happen, and sometimes humor erupts after it happens.

In his book *Let Your Life Speak*, Parker Palmer recalls such an experience. For him the "therapist" was rather a "clearness committee," a practice of Quakers where a group of trusted friends help one sort out a major decision by spending a long evening asking honest open questions to help a person discern one's inner truth.

Parker had requested clearness on whether he should accept the presidency of a small higher education institution, a decision he thought almost certainly was "yes." The first questions were easy. Then another, which seemed even easier, "What would you like most about being a president?" He later recognized that question "lowered me into my heart." He began by telling what he would not like—giving up writing and teaching, the politics, the fundraising, and much more. He went on and on, and the original question was raised again, what would he like? Finally, in a small voice, he admitted, "I guess what I'd like most is getting my picture in the paper with the word *president* under it."

He recalls that though his answer was laughable, no one in this kindly group laughed but rather went into "a long and serious silence, a silence in which I could only sweat and inwardly groan." Eventually this person asked another question, "'Parker, can you think of an easier way to get your picture in the paper?'" He recalls that question "cracked all of us up—and cracked me open." He recognized that the ecology of his life pointed to other gifts and callings. And so he turned down the presidency.[13]

Still another opportunity is celebrating a breakthrough or decision or achievement in the counseling relationship. For example, I once worked—doing mostly vocational counseling—with a woman who had been divorced, depressed, and out of work. In time she interviewed well and was hired in a competitive market. "Wonderful!" I told her. "You must be very happy and your family must be very proud." She looked shocked at my response and then puzzled. "No," she responded. "My family expects that—they're down on me when I don't measure up to that." It was an "aha" moment for both of us. We had a good time laughing and rejoicing at her significant growth.

13. Palmer, *Let Your Life Speak*, 45–46.

I once had a few chuckles over another aspect of counseling—confidentiality. For many years I worked with a couple who approached getting married and then (usually at the male's hesitancy) would pull back. At last, eight years after they started going together, they were finally getting married. Their circle of friends and mine somewhat overlapped. And so, at the wedding rehearsal picnic, person after person would come up to greet me and say, "Wow, you and Bruce and Jene had quite a journey!" All I could answer was "Yes, we did." And then I needed to be silent.

It was awkward at first. Then it hit me that the couple could talk about their relationship and their counseling with their friends, and their friends could talk about it with each other. But I—who know a great deal about this subject—ethically could not. After a while, this strange limit imposed by my professional commitment to confidentiality began to amuse me. I just sat back, chuckling at the partial stories bouncing around together with my self-imposed silence, and had a wonderful time.

With the groom's permission, I couldn't resist kidding him a bit the next day in the wedding service. I recalled a news story about a man in his seventies, who proposed to his lady friend in her sixties. They had "dated" for more than fifty years. When asked why he was so slow with the proposal, the woman replied "Well, he is a little shy, you know." I told Bruce he didn't set a record, but he came close. That much could be told!

Still another area—it is said that a counselor should have a "tolerance for ambiguity." I take that to mean that there are times we don't know what a person is actually saying, or what we are doing, or all the levels on which a topic is being addressed, but we go on. I remember one such time. When I was a youth minister, a shy teenage girl who walked by the church on the way home from school would stop by to visit with me once in a while. One time, when she talked at length, I realized I had totally lost her train of thought. She was speaking hesitantly, slowly, in sentences that made no sense to me at all. It occurred to me that maybe she didn't know how to conclude and leave. I was about to help her say goodbye, when, instead, she said, "Boy this is interesting! I never said these things before." When she left, I had to smile—ambiguity indeed. I was grateful that, on that day at least, I was a little help to someone in spite of myself.

When I was in clinical pastoral education, our supervisor, Les Potter told us another "tolerance for ambiguity" story. A student chaplain was assigned a call on a new patient. Immediately upon entering her room, the various smells nauseated him, and he feared he would throw up. Using his Boy Scout training, he threw himself down in the nearest chair and put his head between his knees. When he could without vomiting, he staggered out the doorway without saying a single word to the patient. To his chagrin, he was sent back to the same patient the next day. He found her sitting up in bed, and she greeted him with a big smile. "Thank you, chaplain for that prayer yesterday. I really needed that!" "That," concluded Potter, "is what you call 'tolerance for ambiguity.'"

Other considerations

At the same time, there are other things to consider. For example, it is wise to be attentive to the counselee's humor and jokes for their "revelatory potential." Jokes, like dreams, can reveal important information that might not be apparent to the one telling it. It may speak of yet unrecognized and unspoken fears, issues, or life complaints.

The client's humor can reveal still other things—it may be a sign that a person is coming out of a time of depression, or that they are feeling more hopeful or powerful. I am always happy when a person, after a painful depression or time of mourning, responds to a quip or originates one with a smile or chuckle. Such is often a sign of hope and progress.

Or the client's humor might signal awareness of a wider range of possible strategies to deal with one's problems. Or, it might just be a joke they heard, enjoyed, and thought they'd pass on. It's good for the counselor to keep one's antennae up, to intuit, wonder, inquire, and explore the patient's expression of humor.

At the same time the pastoral counselor is well advised to be in touch with one's own use of humor. Humor should only be used with counselees we like. Not only that, it should communicate our liking and recognition of our growing rapport with each other before and during the humor.

Such counselor humor might be self-humor about my own problems. It might express a sympathetic understanding of the counselee's occasional frustration with me or with the pace of the therapy. Perhaps some joke will become an "in-joke" between the two of us, a sort of code word for a key issue.

For example, Capps relates the story of a counselor's sessions with an intelligent man, stymied by his obsessive reflections / rationalizations / interpretations. In attempting to cut through all this rumination, the counselor came up with this joke—"A dog was playing along a railroad track, and a train came by and cut off a piece of his tail. The dog was very upset by the situation and sat down on the track and contemplated what life would be like with a shorter tail . . . As he was sitting and ruminating, an express train came along and killed the dog."[14]

> "Dear Mom and Dad,
>
> "I am sorry that I have not written, but all my stationery was destroyed when the dorm burned down. I am now out of the hospital and the doctor said that I will be fully recovered soon. I have moved in with the boy who rescued me, since most of my things were destroyed in the fire.
>
> "Oh yes, I know that you have always wanted a grandchild, so you will be pleased to know that I am pregnant, and you will have one soon.
>
> "Love, Mary
>
> "P.S. There was no fire, my health is perfectly fine, and I am not pregnant. In fact, I do not even have a boyfriend.
>
> "However, I did get a D in French and a C in math and chemistry, and I just wanted to make sure that you keep it all in perspective." (told many times, including in Klein, *The Healing Power of Humor*, 13–14.)

Each time the patient would fall again into this obsessive ruminating behavior, the counselor would say, "You're sitting on the track again." Eventually this led them to be able to move beyond this behavior and into a new phase of therapy.

Sensitivity and limitation

Consideration also needs to be given to the frailty of the client. Pastoral counselor Lloyd Rediger described pastoral care / counseling as "structured intimacy." While the counselee may feel relaxed and free to talk about any painful or sensitive issues, the caregiver does not have the same freedom

14. Capps, *A Time to Laugh*, 136. He is quoting Grossman, "The Use of Jokes in Psychotherapy," 150.

to talk about one's own similar issues. Therefore, humor that might fly with friends may not be fitting. Thomas Kuhlman warns of the dangers of "nonempathic use of humor."

He gives an example from his own practice. He was counseling with a fragile young man named John. The young man was talking of a coming evening with a male friend, and possible places they might go. He mentioned a dancehall. "You know, a lot of neat girls go there. Sometimes they ask the guys to dance! If I made a fool of myself there, I know I'd want to just jump out of the window." The therapist lightly responded, "Well, if you do, put if off until our next session, and I'll let you use one of the windows in my building here. It would probably work better here anyway; we're seven stories off the ground." John went on inventorying possible social outlets and selected a plan, but the spontaneity between them seemed slightly troubled.

However, only when John cancelled the next appointment, did not show up for the rescheduled appointment, and finally reappeared, did they confront what happened. John admitted that he felt that Kuhlman was being a little sarcastic and that he, John was perhaps being too sensitive. A bit of understanding emerged, but he did not come back for further sessions.[15]

Strong friendships may include rough-and-tumble humor and can survive the humor getting out of bounds occasionally. A delicate counseling relationship probably cannot. The counselor's constant question about humor needs to be its potential appropriateness and helpfulness for the client.

First- and second-order reframing

We consider one more contribution of humor before closing this chapter. Donald Capps speaks of humor as an aid to "reframing" (a topic we introduced briefly in chapter 3). This approach takes a term from photography. As one who greatly enjoys photography, this is a playful and helpful image for me. Through my single lens reflex camera, I can "reframe"—do a close up or wide angle, and then at the photo shop, I can again reframe to see and highlight what I most want and to cut out what I don't want. After that, a picture can be "reframed" further by the type of style and material of an outer frame and inner border I select. This gives

15. Capps, *A Time to Laugh*, 145–46. Here he is reflecting on insights from Kuhlman, *Humor and Psychotherapy*, 92.

endless possibilities to each camera shot. Counselors apply this concept to human dilemmas. An incident can be given greater significance (like my counselee's getting a new job) or smaller (a seeming tragedy put into perspective). Counselors attempt to help counselees "think about things differently" or "see a new point of view" or "take other factors into consideration" or "generate more options."

Beyond that, Capps notes that reframing may well effect *second-order change.* He reminds us of the insight that there are two kinds of change: *first-order change* that occurs within some system that remains unchanged; and *second-order change* that alters the system as well. While not always needed, *second-order change* is the deeper and more profound. The system—whatever system that may be—is changed as well as the person within it. It is *change of change.*

He illustrates this with a story far removed from counseling. During a riot in Paris in the nineteenth century, an army commander was ordered to "clear a city square by firing at the rabble." And so he ordered his troops into formation, and told them to take up firing positions. In this frightened and tense situation, the commander "drew his sword and shouted at the top of his lungs: 'Ladies and gentlemen, I have orders to fire at the rabble. But as I see a great number of honest, respectable citizens before me, I request that they leave so that I can safely shoot the rabble.' The square was empty in a few minutes."[16]

How is this second order change? The commander had an order to oppose hostility with counter-hostility, which only would have inflamed the conflict even more. But the commander reframes. He takes the situation outside the framework that up to that time had defined all of them. He sees the crowd not as "rabble" but as "honest, respectable citizens" that he would not want to harm. The threat is averted and hostility reduced, not inflamed.

Reframing—perhaps that is another term for some of what the distinctively Christian pastoral counselor has to offer. When the Bible speaks of "a still more excellent way" (1 Cor 12:31) and "new creation" (2 Cor. 5:17), when it speaks of hope for the fearful, joy in the midst of suffering, and grace for all including the least deserving, it bears witness to second order change of the highest degree. Once in a while we get to

16. Capps, *A Time to Laugh*, 151–52. He is quoting the originators of the theory of first and second order change—Watzlawick, Weakland, and Fisch, *Change: Principles of Problem Formation and Problem Resolution*, 81.

see the triumph of this Spirit in people's lives. That is our privilege. How can we not laugh?

QUESTIONS FOR PERSONAL AND GROUP REFLECTION

1. When, if ever, has humor been helpful to you in the following (either in the giving or the receiving)?
    a. pastoral care in general
    b. pre-marriage counseling and weddings
    c. death, bereavement, funerals and memorial services?
2. Are there any times when as a caregiver, humor was not helpful, or when you regret your use of humor? If so, what were those occasions? What did you learn from the experience?
3. When / if you go for counseling, what humor qualities do you hope for in your counselor? What humor techniques would feel ok to you? What not?
4. What stories do you have to tell about humor in pastoral care—either as caregiver or care receiver?
5. Which, if any, of the list of humor methods mentioned on page 107 would you be most likely to use? Which, if any would you want to avoid?
6. What did this chapter leave out? What would you add to this discussion of humor and pastoral care / counseling?
7. As we continue this exploration, what are you learning about yourself and your spiritual practice of humor?

7

The Baptist Cat and the Presbyterian Dog

(Humor When the People of God Gather)

No discerning person can stand in this place . . . [leading worship and preaching] without a deep sense of awe and responsibility. It is also true that no one should stand in this place without a deep sense of humility and a healthy sense of humor.

—Thomas Long[1]

In this chapter our focus is on times when people gather—worship, preaching, and various small groups including Bible study, Christian education, and formation.

WORSHIP

Near the end of World War II and the end of his life, William Temple, Archbishop of Canterbury, gave a talk on a 1944 BBC broadcast. Surveying the tragic conflict and destruction all around him, he concluded that the world could be saved by one thing only—worship. He then went on to say what he meant by worship. His description has been treasured and quoted again and again ever since.

"To worship is

- to quicken the conscience by the holiness of God,
- to purge the imagination by the beauty of God,
- to open the heart to the love of God, and

1. Long, *The Witness of Preaching*, 8.

- to devote the will to the purpose of God."[2]

Some years before that, in her classic book on worship, Evelyn Underhill began with these words, "Worship, in all its grades and kinds, is the response of the creature to the Eternal."[3]

Worship is a twofold endeavor. It is the human aspiration / attempt to be in touch with God and to offer the praise and adoration due our Creator and Redeemer. It is also the divine encountering us humans and bringing forth wholeness, healing, joy, gratitude and transformed consciences, imaginations, hearts, and wills. As Temple and Underhill pointed out, worship is a life-changing, world-changing experience.

Is there any room for humor within worship—this holy and awesome activity? Does the God whose nature we considered in chapter five allow, expect, and anticipate that humor and laughter will occur in worship?

While some worship is a solitary encounter—one believer "alone with the Alone,"—more often it takes place when people gather. The variety of settings and ways that people worship is vast and amazing. Some worship in tiny groups, and others gather by the thousands. Some have a revered country church or tiny chapel, some a home, storefront, or school, and others gather in vast auditoriums or stately cathedrals. Some value silence and meditation and others embrace enthusiastic praise, the louder and more rhythmic the better.

Those who regularly lead worship and / or preach need a combination of several spiritual practices: prayer, including prayerful anticipation and preparation; deep systematic study and thoughtful design;—and humor? If so, how does the spiritual practice of humor contribute to this important church leadership function? Let's explore.

Accidental humor

There are at least two things that all these styles of worship have in common: they are regular, frequent, customary activities; and they are led by very human—and thus fallible—people. These folks lead and participate in worship week in and week out, tired and alert, eager and reluctant, fully alive to the experience and dulled by habit.

2. Temple, 1944 BBC Broadcast.
3. Underhill, *Worship*, 339, quoted in White *Introduction to Christian Worship*, 19.

Thus, whether we choose to include humor or not, it is likely that mishaps and unintended humor will creep in from time to time and make its presence known. My friend and colleague, homiletics professor Mike Graves tells his classes to be aware of the "dancing bears"[4] that appear in almost every worship service. That is the unexpected, the unavoidable—all those things that will detract, distract, and disrupt the solemn pursuit of worship.

Here are a few examples of times when such humor accidentally happened. Some of these are from my experience, and others were related by friends:

- I led worship in a chapel built into a hill. On one side, the windows were at ground level with window wells. One Sunday morning, a neighborhood tabby cat, who must have found a favorite place for napping in the sun, crawled into the window well (outside), luxuriously gave itself a "cat bath" and then curled up to nap in full sight of the gathered worshippers. So enchanted and amused was the congregation that a worship team member suggested having a different "guest animal" every week.
- Tom Long recalls another "animal experience." During his childhood, his family worshipped in a small Presbyterian church in rural Georgia. In the heat of summer with all windows and doors open, a "stray hound of indecipherable lineage" sometimes found his way into worship. Ushers were unable to control him, so they accommodated the dog's presence. This "invasion" delighted the children, while being mostly ignored by the adults. He recalls, "Whatever else it may mean, a dog loose in worship unmasks all pretense and undermines false dignity." Looking back he sees the hound's presence as a parable, that of "a hound absurdly loose in their midst and a gathering of frail human beings astonishingly saved by the grace of God . . ." If the young ministers who competed with the dog for attention saw that, says Long, ". . . in some deep and silent place within them, they were surely taken with rich and cleansing laughter—and if they were, they were better preachers of the gospel for it."[5]

4. A quote from Dillard, *Teaching a Stone to Talk*, 31–32.

5. Long, *The Witness of Preaching*, 9–10.

- A minister was about to begin the evening service when his three-year-old daughter escaped from his wife. For some reason, the little girl must have been greatly upset with her father. He stood behind the pulpit to give the call to worship, but before he could, his tiny daughter ran up to right in front of him and yelled, "Liar, liar, liar!"
- I had somewhat better experience with a child dominating the attention of the worshippers. When our youngest daughter, Laurie, was about one, I had been gone to a denominational meeting for the weekend and came back just in time to conduct worship on Sunday morning. Her mother was holding her during that service. Apparently while I was behind the pulpit on a fairly high platform, she did not see me. But when I came down and stood on congregational level for the closing hymn, she spied me and reached out, crying loudly to be released to me. After the benediction I walked by, took her from my wife, and held her while I greeted worshippers. I was told that whatever else happened in worship that day was quickly forgotten. Our beautiful baby daughter upstaged it all. (That was her and my day. Life being what it is, the recriminations and challenges would inevitably come later.)
- Indeed, the involvement of children in worship, whether at a story time or for services of dedication or baptism of infants brings many opportunities of unexpected delight and laughter for worshippers. Bob Parrott recalls a time when he was baptizing a baby. The baby's four-year-old sister was standing beside her parents for this ritual. This child began to show some discomfort at the proceedings. Dr. Parrott bent over and asked the four-year-old girl "Is something troubling you?" The child looked up with a frown on her face, and speaking loud enough for all to hear, responded, "My little sister does not liked to be passed around to everyone everywhere." The congregation laughed. In the light of comments he received later, Parrott recognized that this was a moment of grace. One worshipper told him, "When you stopped in the middle of that service, when the whole congregation stopped and gave attention to that one little child, it made me realize like never before, how God gives every one of us . . . undivided attention."[6]

6. Parrott, *God's Sense of Humor*, 106.

- In a similar vein, my former pastor, Heather Entrekin, recalls, "In telling the children the story of Moses once, I asked a child to volunteer to be Moses. She did and obediently took off her shoes when we got to Holy Ground. A reader from the balcony with a voice like God had a speaking part, and this unnerved her. As we approached the burning bush she said, 'I don't want to be Moses any more.' I responded, 'That's OK. Moses didn't want to be Moses either.' And we put her shoes back on and continued."
- I was present when Ron Erickson conducted his very first worship service with a congregation to which had been recently called. He was approaching the climax of his sermon when a light fixture in the sanctuary began to shake and then fell with a loud crash. There were three such fixtures, and fortunately the one that fell was the only one not above the pews where the worshippers were seated.

> A cleric about to begin the liturgy, tapped the microphone to see if it was "live." He turned to an assistant and mistakenly commented, "There's something wrong with this microphone." The well-trained congregation responded, "And also with you."

Ron was stopped, stunned, breathless, and speechless for a moment. He could only get out a "Wow, I'll have something to write my parents about this week." He looked up and saw a bit of smoke coming from the place where the light fixture had been. "Does that need attention?" he asked. Someone shook his head "no." "Well," Ron went on, "Good luck out there." And he went on to the short conclusion of his sermon.

- Sometimes the "dancing bear" is the slips of our own tongues. I recall a Youth Sunday. One young person who was to give the opening part of a several-person sermon panicked at the last minute and begged to be released from this task. The sermon theme was "Thy Kingdom Come on Earth." His was the first part, "Unless one is born of water and the spirit, one shall not see the kingdom . . ." A young pastor, I "winged it" trying to provide enough introduction to give continuity to the youths' other sermons. I meant to say, "I recently stood by when a baby was born. A baby contributes nothing to its own birth. A baby is born by the labor of its mother and the skill of its doctor." Instead I said, "A baby is born by the labor of its mother and the skill of its *father*!" The moment quickly passed without too much notice (at least I hoped so). However, after the service, a few men my age asked me if I were going to offer classes on that skill.

- Marcus McFaul recalls a slip, when, instead of using the word "enemies" he suggested "we should make our enemas our friends." He thought he'd escaped notice until one elderly member smilingly told him, "Enemas are already my friend."
- Both of us got by a little better than the famous preacher / theologian William Willimon. He recalls a time, when overcome by jet lag and trying to live up to the hype of the one who introduced him, he asked in a loud firm voice "And what is the most significant event our faith has to offer?" He bellowed his answer, "The erection." Though he went on to say "I mean the resurrection," and though he said the right word at least a dozen times, no one seemed to notice. As he put it "Church was out." One woman told him, "I'm sure I shall remember your sermon for the rest of my life." He could hear her laughing as she walked out of the building.[7]

How does one exercise the spiritual practice of humor when such things happen? The graceful wisdom is simply to relax, enjoy the fun, and join in the laughter. If I am the one who "messed up," self humor is an important part of my practice—helpful to me and appreciated by others. If others accidentally caused the misstep, quiet acceptance is in order, not embarrassing them. Then lead the congregation back into the holy mysteries of worship. Be aware that the humor may provide respite in the arduous task of worship, or, by the grace of God, it may be part of the means by which worship is experienced.

Pranks and intrusions

There is another aspect to consider as well. Some people might see a worship service as a place to pull off a prank with the intent of adding some fun—or disruption or whatever—to the proceedings. How should

7. Willimon, "Sermon Slips," 19.

a worship leader respond on such occasion? Again, a few such situations come to mind.

- One of my friends was an associate minister in a large and rather proper congregation. Like most Baptist churches, at communion services they served unfermented (very sweet) grape juice. At one communion service, he and the senior pastor were co-leading. When the minister bid people drink, the two clergy looked at each other in sheer terror. They were aware that they were drinking a very strong, sour, red wine. This would have stirred quite an uproar. However, as they looked over the congregation, the people all seemed to be undisturbed, in the quiet, prayerful, pensive mood that is often experienced at that moment in worship. They later learned that some impish deacon had managed so that only the two ministers were served the fermented wine. Everyone else was provided for, as usual.
- John Blythe was conducting the beloved, traditional, and well-attended "Christmas on Campus" service at the church-related college where he was chaplain. When he announced the opening carol and people took up the hymnbooks, there was loud clatter all over the chapel. Unknown culprits had placed a table knife in the middle of every hymnal. Though John was seething, the president of the college laughed, and John let it pass. The rest of the service continued without other incident.
- Once, at the moment before a wedding was to start, I came to the room where the groom and attendants were waiting. I found them passing a flask of whisky around, completely against church policy, which they well knew. They put it away, and I decided to let it pass. Just before entering the sanctuary, I asked the best man if he had the ring the groom would give the bride, and he assured me he did. When we came to the point in the ceremony where I asked for the ring, the best man pulled out empty pockets and shrugged, as did each groomsman in turn. Finally the last groomsman held up a ring box. He then threw it—from the congregational level to the platform level—thirty feet or so, to the best man. After the service, I heard the father of the groom congratulate these men—fraternity brothers of the groom—for making it the funniest wedding he'd ever attended. Weddings seem to stir pranks—within the service

> and afterward. Another minister told me of a wedding where he feared the worst out of pre-marriage counseling and had his fears confirmed. The groom walked down the aisle wearing pink shoes. After the pronouncement, this groom took out a pair of handcuffs and put them on his bride and himself. In still another wedding, there was an incident reported to me by the church's wedding hostess. (In that congregation we had a practice of allowing other pastors and wedding parties to use our sanctuary). This particular wedding group brought in a huge sound system and for the recessional cranked up, "Another One Bites The Dust!"

When such events happen, what does a worship leader who is also attempting the spiritual practice of humor do? Such tricks may be playful and harmless. Even if inappropriate, it is prudent to be a good sport, let it happen and pass without encouraging it, and go on. This occurrence may in some strange way enrich the event. If not, it is good to let it go. That is what the pastors did in the first two of these incidents. (John later discovered that it was his own daughter and her fiancé who planned and pulled off the "knife prank.")

I didn't do very well with the wedding ring incident. As a matter of fact, I failed to follow my own (belated) wisdom on this. While I said nothing to the perpetrators, at the wedding reception I was asked by the people at the table where we were seated what I thought of the groomsmen's little joke. With rather tight lips, I responded that with all the thoughtful work the bride had done to prepare the ceremony and setting, it would be too bad if the prank was what we remembered from this wedding. Another person at the table responded, "He (referring to me) doesn't like for people to have fun in the sanctuary." Though the groomsmen were inappropriate, I could have done better, much better. If I could have stayed a little lighter, I would not have given this minor incident more significance than it deserved. I still had more to learn about this practice of humor, such as laughing when I—or my leadership or service—is in some way the victim of the joke.

The entertainer / liturgist?

This practice of humor I advocate is for one's own health, joy, resilience. While its purpose is not performance or entertaining, sometimes the joy will spill over in the presence of others and is enjoyed by all. That, however, is not its main purpose.

In exploring this practice, I caution against something that appears to be similar but really is quite different—the minister who thinks s/he *has* to be funny while leading worship. These clergy force something that is not naturally there. They seem to think the worship of God is not enough; there has to be entertainment as well.

I am recalling such a time. Some years ago, as new neighbors were moving in next door, they put a large sign on the front lawn, "Glenn and Jenny are getting married this afternoon at five. Come on by."

A couple dozen of us—folks living nearby and some coworkers—responded and came as invited to meet our new neighbors and to be present for their wedding vows. Glenn and Jenny were both late midlife people, divorced and with young adult children. They had picked their church in our community and invited one of the clergy on the staff there to officiate.

This young clergy person seemed to think a simple outdoor wedding on a back patio had to be funny. As part of the wedding meditation this minister told a series of jokes about weddings of very old people, including the one about the old man who married, not for companionship, romance, or finances, but "because she can drive at night." These jokes were insulting to older people and certainly to a midlife couple with a vigorous romantic, sexual love for each other. They wanted a wedding on their day of moving in together to start this chapter of their life with dignity and integrity. That was what Glenn told me during over-the-fence visiting in the months following. From my perspective, a simple, reverent wedding, celebrating the new beginning and new life of this couple would have been much more fitting.

As I attend worship in various settings, from time to time I experience a similar attitude in the worship leader. Whether it fits or not there will be jokes, quips, something of the master of ceremonies style of worship leadership. It often comes across as forced, self-centered, and uncertain of what worship is or why people come to worship, fearful that people won't be pleased or satisfied. Humor is superimposed upon worship rather than a fitting expression of some of the truly joyful aspects of worship.

I would hope for such leaders that they could discover more deeply what worship means in their faith tradition, why people worship, and how to lead people into these holy mysteries. Then, possible humor within worship might come more naturally. And, if it doesn't, that's ok too.

Humorous worship and worshipful humor?

We continue to explore—is there room for humor within the holy and awesome activity of worship? For the person engaging the spiritual practice of humor, can that humor be authentically expressed in fitting worship? If so, when and how?

The answer hinges on our concept of God and our theology of worship. In chapter five, I summarized what I trust is a faithful interpretation of the God revealed in the Bible. We saw God's laughter in creation, God's derisive laughter when we ignore or deny our place in God's plan, and God's victorious laughter in redeeming us. Divine humor is reflected in human joy, hope, and grace.

The God thus described loves and delights in creation and in us creatures, with all our quirks and frailties. This is a God to be praised and celebrated with singing, instruments, dance, and with great joy and laughter.

This expression of a theology of humor in worship is seen in a centuries old tradition known as "The Easter Laugh" or "Day of Joy and Laughter." While the precise origin of this practice is not known, William D. Webber intuitively imagines its beginning:

"It began hundreds of years ago. A monk, whose name has been lost in history, was pondering the meaning of the events of holy week, with its solemn observances . . . , and the astonishing, earth-shaking events of Easter. 'What a surprise ending,' he thought. Then suddenly, like a bolt of lightning, he had a new thought. His hearty laugh startled his fellow monks, breaking the silence of their contemplation.

"'Don't you see,' he cried, 'It was a joke! A great joke! The best joke in all history! On Good Friday, when Jesus was crucified, the devil thought he had won. But God had the last laugh on Easter when he raised Jesus from the dead.'"[8]

The idea spread rapidly in Orthodox, Catholic, and Protestant churches. The Fellowship of Merry Christians has recently urged more widespread observance of God's great "practical joke." These services are often held either on Easter Monday or the Sunday after Easter.

8. Webber, "What Do You Do The Day After Easter?"

A friend gave me the account of such an occasion in a Wichita, Kansas, Mennonite Church, the fifth year they have held such an event. Co-pastor Tom Harder began this service by saying, "Today we want to celebrate the resurrection through humor, laughter, and uninhibited joy." The Bible verse on the cover of the bulletin was Job 8:21, "He will yet fill your mouth with laughter and your lips with shouts of joy."

Small groups performed "takeoffs" of *Sound of Music* songs. "The Pews are Alive with the Sound of Mennonites," "How Do You Solve a Problem Like the Budget?" and "These are a Few of My Favorite Names." A skit featured a panel rating the best juice for communion and, to their embarrassment, discovered they had selected "Real-Value Artificial Grape Drink from Walmart." The collection of loose change for the Mennonite Central Committee was enlivened by "Chuting the Loot" which involved lining up several sections of guttering from the balcony to the center aisle below and sliding the coins into a bucket. Attendance was well above average, which indicated that this unusual service in a Mennonite church had gained acceptance over the years. At the close of the service, co-pastor Lois Harder dismissed the congregation with these words, "Take this holy hilarity with you into a world that is sad and needs the laughter of faith and joy."[9]

Such a service is quite probably not for everyone (and this type of celebration could take many forms), but it does claim and express a significant theological truth—that joy and rejoicing, with laughter, are fitting responses to God's lavish and surprising redemption. After such a time, one cannot approach worship the weeks after that in quite the same old way.

As you may have noticed, there is at least an apparent inconsistency between the previous section of this chapter and this one. Don't force humor in worship, but plan a service of Easter laughter? The worship leader should not feel constrained to entertain but should authentically claim the joy of resurrection faith with clapping, singing, dancing, and laughing? How do this caution and this encouragement come together?

In all honesty, I must answer, "imperfectly." Humor is in the eye and ear of each of us, and we see / hear it differently. What one person may experience as forced or phony in worship may be welcome relief and enjoyment for another. A service of Easter laughter may not be for everyone (it's been rumored that some of them are rather raucous!) but

9. Schrag, "Holy Humor," 1, 6. Thanks to Robert J. Carlson for sharing this piece.

it may help the promise of the faith to sink home with others. We will have differences in culture and custom on this as well.

In attempting to live with both the caution and the encouragement, a few guidelines are in order. Here are some simple but basic ways to invite our practice of humor into worship:

- Relax more. Go with the flow of worship. God can use our mistakes and mishaps, and our great God is not undone by our childish pranks. Our incarnate Lord who loved children with all their playfulness and laughter is honored when our joy erupts into laughter along with the children.
- Smile, enjoy. Laugh along with the others at the inevitable unexpected happenings. At least two of us among those surveyed were often reminded by spouses and members not to frown so much, but to look like leading worship was an enjoyable experience. I confess that sometimes people worshipping under my leadership didn't know how much I was enjoying this privilege—they couldn't tell it from my "poker face." (Good grief, does a poker face belong in worship?).
- Find a balance between two extremes. Avoid the "I must entertain" mentality. But also avoid the rigidity that asserts that there is no place for intended humor—or unintended humor—in worship.
- Pastors surveyed noted that announcement time—whether at the beginning of the service or at its conclusion was often a time when humor, good news, relaxation, and celebration could be brought very explicitly into the community experience.
- Be who you are (a theme to which we will return) and be a part of the faith and liturgical heritage to which you belong. However, also dare to find ways to stretch and tweak it.

Playful ritual?

Robert Fulghum tells of attempting to lead his Unitarian congregation into a new alternate ritual that would offer and celebrate the search for community that he sees as a key element in observing the Lord's Supper. Over the years, he tried varied ways. Once he passed out tangerines—one for every three or four people. One was to peel the tangerine, another distribute it, another care for peels and seeds. This innovation had no groundswell of support, so he experimented with other elements. These included animal crackers, Gummi Bears, jelly beans, M&M's (which, contrary to advertising do melt in your hands). He recalls the "all-time lulu" was "Pop Rocks" a candy loaded with carbon dioxide that sort of explodes when you bite on it, producing stained tongues and lips. ("What happened to your mouth?" "I went to church on the wrong Sunday.")

Years later, as he reflected on these experiments, he discerns these insights:

First, as these partially-successful experiments show, it is difficult to construct new rituals on top of well-established tradition. But second, the congregation understood what he as minister was seeking and wanted the same thing—ritual acts to express authentic community. "Finally, all these wiggy attempts produced a great deal of laughter and will long be fondly remembered and recounted by members of the congregation . . . This laughter is holy. You'll never convince me that Jesus and his companions did not also laugh together, even at the final supper."[10]

Fulghum and his Unitarian flock may have felt freer to play with rituals that others of us often experience as both more formal and fully formed. Still, it is fitting to ask, what is the range of meanings in every Christian ritual act, and what are the opportunities for celebration and play within it?

PREACHING

And what about humor in that aspect of worship that is almost always included—the sermon or homily?

A specific, developed view—comedy and preaching

Joseph Webb offers much wisdom and reflection about this in his fine book, *Comedy and Preaching.*[11] Aware that there are theological, biblical, ethical, and practical resistances to humor in the pulpit, he counters by pointing to the theological validity and rhetorical contributions of humor. In this he quotes and agrees with Chad Walsh that a "great part of the malaise afflicting Christianity today, particularly in its Protestant forms is that it has forgotten (or never learned) how to laugh.'"[12]

10. Fulghum, *From Beginning to End*, 83–88.

11. Webb, *Comedy and Preaching.*

12. Ibid., 17.

What is a comic sermon? Webb responds that it is not defined in terms of its laugh quotient. It is possible to preach a comic sermon that does not induce any overt laughter. The purpose "is to nourish, explicate, encourage, and celebrate both sides of that very human / divine, divine / human coin. The sermon that embraces this dual struggle—of God in human form and human searching as divine activity—becomes part of that divine comedy with its fully human cast."[13]

This type of sermon expresses the comic spirit which has at least five major dimensions: (1) immanence, particularly a focus on "human relationship as the essence of all life and being"; (2) doubting—a freedom and drive to examine and question everything; (3) incongruity—exploring disparities in all life and interaction, with an awareness of life's basic irony; (4) a drive to create and sustain ambiguity (for example, to blur the distinction between hero and villain); and (5) a basic and underlying goal of promoting human (including social) equality and solidarity.[14]

> "The kind of humor I like is the thing that makes me laugh for five seconds and think for ten minutes."—William Davis
>
> "My method is to take the utmost trouble to find the right thing to say, and then say it with the utmost levity."—George Bernard Shaw
>
> "What I want to do is make people laugh so that they'll see things seriously."—William K. Zinsser

Therefore, a comic sermon needs to have certain qualities. It must have a clear purpose and direction, something to say. Laughter cannot be the purpose of the sermon, but a contributor to the sermon's purpose.

This kind of sermon will encompass a wider range of emotions in complex relationship to each other—rather like an episode of M*A*S*H. It is this-worldly; while vitally interested in theology, the quest of this sermon is to explore what our theology actually is as we live it out day by day.

The preacher of such a comic sermon takes the inspired Bible also as an authentically human book, and views God's actions as described in the Bible as a comic play, full of surprise turns and even more surpris-

13. Ibid., 36.

14. Ibid., 21, 21–28.

ing endings (all in keeping with how we discovered humor in the Bible in chapter four). The comic sermon will unfailingly speak of hope and hopefulness. It will point to and affirm that on which our hope stands.

Further, this type of sermon will build and encourage connecting and bonding—preacher with congregation, worshippers with each other, and people with God. "The bond that comedy or the sharing of laughter, makes possible is unlike any other bond that can tie human beings together."[15]

The bedrock of comic preaching is story and storytelling. Stories can embody a truth without the truth having to be elaborated. Stories also invite the hearers into a shared experience. Further, stories can impact behavior by holding up ways to do something or actions to avoid. The end of a good story can have a "go and do likewise" effect without it ever being spoken.

If stories are to be effective, they are to be told about others, not the preacher. The minister is not to be the hero or the villain. Also, a good storyteller lets the story carry its own impact. One should not become "preachy" or "moralistic" about what the story means after it is told.[16]

The search for new and stimulating story should be a constant for the preacher. While not all of us have the eyes to see the entertaining in the midst of the mundane in the manner of an Erma Bombeck, Anne Lamott, Dave Barry, or Garrison Keeler, we can move in that direction. Watching, observing, overhearing, taking notes, journalizing can all lead to a reserve of story that is available for sermons. An otherwise nondescript event can be abbreviated, or expanded, or detail-added to make a story out of it. "True" and "factual" are not necessarily synonyms!

Webb suggests that the comic premise is the principle of incongruity—both finding and creating things that do not, should not, and usually don't go together. This may lead to "perspective by incongruity." There are many forms of incongruity to be explored: the anticipated and the unanticipated; human ambition and human achievement—or perhaps desire and achievement; the ideal and the actual; the individual and the institution; the normal in juxtaposition with the abnormal. When we see these in others, we see ourselves more clearly as well.

Professional comedians address such incongruities with the devices of hyperbole and exaggeration. In so doing, they create a new and unex-

15. Ibid., 45. These paragraphs have summarized 37–45.

16. Ibid., 62–63.

pected incongruity. Another method is word play of various kinds. This may vary from the pun to a careful literal scrutiny of something said or written. (We found these very humor tactics in the Bible.) These methods are available to the preacher as well, but Webb cautions that they should be used cautiously, perhaps underused rather than overused.[17]

A central ingredient of the comic sermon is the use of metaphor, which, he points out, is what every good English teacher has told us for generations, "A metaphor is a figure of speech used to explain something unfamiliar by something familiar."[18] The Bible contains a number of metaphors that may be quite helpful. However, in addition, the preacher is well-advised to seek and create new metaphors that will help congregation see things in a new light. It is ok to venture metaphors that may be risky or funny at times.

How does one address the biblical text in the comic sermon? The preacher may well bring playful inquiry and imagination to the text. One might come to the text with naivety asking all sorts of "simple questions" about it. Or one might note how brief and cryptic the text and imaginatively add details to make the story more vivid. Or one might carry on a dialogue with the scripture. Again, one might transpose it from "then" to "now" and from "there" to "here."

I have summarized Webb at length because he brings together one's spiritual practice of humor and the task of sermon preparation / delivery so beautifully. Approach scripture aware of all the humorous literary devices you find there; view life with the eyes of a comic, as well. In the pulpit share what has arisen out of that life practice of humor.

Perhaps your interest is aroused by my brief summary and you will want to read his book, a complete treatment of comedy and preaching. I am grateful to him for a strong, clear, articulate theology and method of comic preaching.

Other perspectives on humorous preaching

However, one style does not fit all. There are many styles of humor in the pulpit, and undoubtedly, some of them are more fitting than others. Let's further reflect for those whose style may not completely fit in that which Webb has described for us thus far.

17. Ibid., 77–94.
18. Ibid., 95.

Burton Howe noted "Phillips Brooks defined preaching as 'Truth through Personality.' Humor might be defined as 'Levity through personality.' Humor needs to be sincere. Otherwise it will be ineffective or worse."[19] I particularly like his phrase, "levity through personality."

Other pastors have told me that while they are urged to tell jokes from the pulpit, for them jokes feel arbitrary and contrived. And, they confess, they are not good joke tellers. Their humor will be more from true stories in their own lives and others. To be authentic, they need to not feel forced to tell jokes.

They are in good company. As a matter of fact, Webb argues against jokes in comic sermons. He says ministers are not very good joke tellers. Jokes superimposed on a sermon by someone not comfortable with joke telling are apt to sound silly and trite.

On the other hand, many of us love good funny stories, including jokes, and these make their way into our sermons sometimes. The key, I believe, is for each of us to find our own voice in humor and our own style of humor, a quest that this book engages.

Another good question to consider is what kind of humor plays well in this community? What do folks in this setting enjoy, encourage, tolerate? What is likely to be offensive or out of bounds here?

As for oneself, a minister may want to review the various types of humor that were listed in chapter two from Evan Esar, then ask oneself, "Which of these do I enjoy the most? Which of these (in all due humility) am I pretty good at? Which of these do I engage to heal, console, encourage, and sustain my own life and ministry? How well do these fit in my public ministry and my present setting? Into what other kinds of humor would I like to stretch a bit?" Such questions may invite the spiritual practice of humor into the tasks of worship leadership and preaching.

That exercise might also reveal that one does not feel capable of humor in public discourse at all. If that happens to be the case for you, we will work on that in chapter nine.

> "As a preacher, Barth could acknowledge that some of his sermons were real clinkers, like the one on the sinking of the Titanic which he later noted was as great a disaster as the original event." (Daniel Migliore, "Reappraising Barth's Theology," 312.)

19. Howe, personal correspondence, response to a questionnaire I circulated.

Whatever the humor methods one chooses or evolves or discovers, or finds emerging, it is good to learn to be able to relax with them. I wholeheartedly concur that revelatory story is the bedrock of effective preaching. When offering such story, I may experience people laughing where I didn't expect and not laughing where I did. Indeed, the little humorous piece or quip or wordplay cleverly-inserted may go unnoticed. I personally have a rather dry sense of humor. So much so, that such comments inserted into sermons often go by without noticeable response from anyone. I have learned to tell myself that if they amused me that is enough (part of my practice of humor). These quips contributed to my enjoyment in preparing the sermon. Any further response is fringe benefit. I should not repeat the statement, hoping for larger response. Or worse yet, I should not explain it. Let it go.

Healthy self humor is often the best choice and fits the image of the preacher as "fool for Christ's sake." I can express my humanity by poking fun at myself, my profession, my national origin, and my struggles as a family member. Even as I do this, I need to honor the dignity and privacy of my family members. Stories about spouse and children should be used only with permission. Indeed stories about any recognizable persons should have prior permission.

Humor and the comic sermon are fitting for a number of occasions, but certainly not all. There are tragic times when the mood of lament must be sounded, occasions of personal, community, or national grief that should be acknowledged and comfort extended.

Even on those occasions, a bit of humor may be appropriate. As my homiletics professor Ed Linn used to point out, delicate humor, carefully used can be a counterbalance to a somber or deep moment, giving the hearers an emotional break before proceeding further with serious matters. This may function like a key change in a piece of music.[20] And the certain sounding of Christian hope, the heartbeat of the Christian faith, while it may not stir even a smile, is the promise of a dawn beyond the present darkness.

One more counsel—before using humor in ministry, it is well to know both our own heart and our relationship with those who will hear the humor. I once heard a borderline off-color joke I thought was uproariously funny. It had to do with a congregation who mistreated a minister who did not respond in kind. However, as he walked out of

20. Recalled by seminary classmate Robert Overstreet in personal correspondence.

the church after the benediction of his final service, he wore a passive-aggressive object that expressed his contempt (a piece of mistletoe on his coat tail).

I repeated this joke several times to minister friends. Some would laugh uproariously, and others would laugh a little, politely, or respond in silence. One minister upon hearing it burst out crying. In retrospect, I see that I did not know myself or my hearers. I did not recognize how hurt and angry I was at the time, and therefore how this joke was a "safe" expression of this hurt. Nor did I always know how my hearers were doing. Clearly, at least one was in great pain and I was no help.

I also recall a Sunday when I preached a sermon I thought was prophetic. With a lot of emotion, I came down pretty hard on the congregation. Afterward, a wise older member asked me, "Do you feel better now?" Her remark drew me up short and helped me realize how much of my unresolved feelings had crept into my sermon. It also stirred in me an amusing picture of the congregation functioning as a Rogerian non-directive counselor for the minister. They just sat there quietly while the minister talked out his feelings and problems. They listened to this immature preacher rant, listened as an understanding parent, or a quiet, peaceful counselor! I could almost hear my friend Lee doing a Bob Newhart routine on this, "I see. You are now using your congregation as your therapist and you are wondering how much to pay them!" I guess we all have our good days and bad, but next time, I had better find a professional counselor.

In learning from this, I need to be in touch with my own spiritual and emotional health or lack of it. Too easily humor can express that lack. Humor out of this attitude may numb my pain for a moment, but it may also inflict greater pain on others. My search is for a humor practice that enhances and enriches one's own and others' spiritual life.

I also need to be sensitive to my relationship with the hearers. Tom Mullen tells of giving a public lecture on humor. He mentioned a newspaper article describing a Roman Catholic Parish in which a drive-in confessional was used. He suggested the practice might be called "toot and tell."

He got a big laugh, but then had a conversation with a Roman Catholic woman afterward. He asked her if she was offended by his joke. She first denied it, but then wrote a letter confessing to at least discomfort. The reason, she said was "I didn't know you or anything about your attitude toward my beloved Holy Mother Church, so I had no way of surmising whether you were laughing *with* us or *at* us." She went on to say that one of the things she loved about her church was its "capacity for laughing at herself and her children. But, laughter from a stranger is not the same comfortable affectionate matter as laughing at one's own foibles and those of one's cherished family members and dear friends."[21]

Mullen concludes that laughing *with* unites and overcomes. But the trust needs to be established so that it is clear we are laughing together. This is true when we are addressing persons outside our religious community. But this trust also needs to be established, maintained, and nourished within the faith communities we serve.

CHRISTIAN EDUCATION AND SMALL GROUPS

When we gather, whether for Christian education pursuits, spiritual growth support or other types of church groups, there are special humor opportunities. There may be less inhibition and greater freedom to experience the power of humor together. This may be the place to begin to claim the power of laughing together.

The spontaneous enjoyment of meeting each other and hearing people's stories is a starting place. People's gifts of humor, whether it is a hearty laugh, or the willingness to tease or be teased, or the irresistible punster can enliven a group. I have provided discussion questions at the end of each chapter in the hope that this book would help groups of people laugh together, and then reflect and grow together.

Or, to consider another example, Doug Adams, one of the Bible scholars we explored, not only discovered humor in scripture. He found ways to let those discoveries influence the way he taught about it. Here are a few of his playful ways to communicate what he has found in scripture:

- When exploring Jesus' genealogy in Matthew, he will bring placards to guide those gathered how to respond to each name in the genealogy. The placards include: CHEERS, HISSES, BOOS, APPLAUSE, and HUH? Participants participate in the genealogy and enjoy the irony.
- With parables, he enters into the story with people. For example, when looking at Luke 15:11–32, he will ask some older man,

21. Mullen, *Laughing Out Loud*, 43–44.

"What would your father have said to you if you asked for your inheritance before he died?" Later he will turn to some man and ask, "You look like you'd know, what is dissolute living?" He notes this, like several other parables, does not really end. In the last scene, the father and son are arguing outside. He invites groups to write alternate endings to the parable. Where does it lead? What are the possibilities?

- In the parable of the "rich fool" Luke 12:16–20, he uses a method called "liquid pictures." He asks for five volunteers, gives each one of them one phrase from the parable to repeat and accompany with a gesture. Each one in turn says their line loudly three times and then continues softly, doing the gesture. The five are "produced abundantly," "pull down," "build larger," "eat drink and be merry," "you fool."
- To demonstrate the satirical image of "log in your eye," he will take a bolster from the back of a sofa and hold it up in front of his eye, bumping into students, making comments such as "I see your difficulty clearly" or "I think my perceptive insights will solve your problem." All the while someone reads Luke 6:41–42.
- He may prepare and use dramatic readings to summarize a lengthy background necessary for understanding a particular biblical episode. Or, he may use drama to illustrate the humor within a passage. For example, he dramatizes Paul's series of rhetorical questions in 1 Cor 6:1–20, with the Corinthians giving first the wrong, then the right answer.[22]

This by no means exhausts his playful methods for using humor while finding and expressing the humor in scripture. Stimulated by his example, we may discover other joyous ways to discover, claim, and embrace the Bible's surprising message. This may enrich our group life even further, and invite still more merriment when we gather as the people of God.

22. Adams, *The Prostitute in the Family Tree*, 4–5, 12–18, 50, 52, 86–89.

QUESTIONS FOR PERSONAL AND GROUP REFLECTION

1. What have been your experiences of humorous mishaps or slips of the tongue within worship?
2. Have you had pranks occur while leading worship? Have you ever precipitated any? What is your view of pranks during worship?
3. What is your response when people tell you jokes about how ministers only work one day a week, and otherwise have it rather easy?
4. What types of humor do you find fitting in worship and in preaching? What types of humor do people in your congregation and community appreciate most? Appreciate least?
5. Where do the spiritual practice of humor and the tasks of worship planning / leadership and preaching come together for you?
6. As we continue this exploration, what are you learning about yourself and your spiritual practice of humor?

8

Laughter When You May Need It Most

(Humor and Administration, Criticism, and Conflicts)

The church is something like Noah's Ark. If it weren't for the storm outside, you couldn't stand the smell inside!

—A Medieval manuscript,
quoted by Robert McAfee Brown.[1]

When my friend (whom I mentioned in the introduction) asked me out for coffee and talk, her pain was about complications in administration and with some of the resistance, criticism, conflicts, and fall out that happened to her. Clearly if there is a place where when both a tough skin and a frequent / constant practice of healthy self-humor is needed, it is when one is a leader in a voluntary association, such as a church.

And so our attention now turns to possible humor in these various administrative and leadership tasks of ministry. We will first glimpse at the everyday tasks of relating as church staff, stewardship / finances, and board meetings. Then, our attention will be given to the topics of controversy, conflict, and criticism.

ADMINISTRATION

When I would complain to my friend Lee Regier (you met him in chapter one) about frustrations with administration, he would playfully respond by pointing to the possible root meaning of that term. "Ad-"

1. Brown, *The Significance of the Church*, 17.

can mean "to, toward, in the direction of, for the purpose of." And the other word is ministry. Administration describes our activities to enlist, recruit, and organize for the purpose of the ministry to which we aspire. Virginia Cetuk offers the imaginative phrase "organizing the love" for administration.

For some, it comes naturally to carry on these responsibilities with joy, enthusiasm, and a sense of fun. For others of us, this is a bigger challenge. I am among the latter group.

Apparently I am not alone. In the survey I did among colleagues in ministry about their humor practices, the fewest responses were in the area of administration. It appeared that these clergy friends also saw this as a necessary, but sometimes very difficult part of their work.

And yet, some saw opportunities for humor even here. Kathy Pickett notes, "During weeks of chaos when it seems like anything that can go wrong does, humor always lightens the load. I often suggest we should create a soap-opera, 'As the Church Turns.'"

CHURCH STAFF

Other ministers mentioned how helpful it is to have church staffs that enjoy each other and have fun while working together. Appreciation of each other, celebrating birthdays and other events in each other's life may enrich trust and partnership. Learning to appreciate—or tolerate—each other's style of humor can enrich one's day and work. Some staff members have the gift of encouraging and calling forth others' humor. One person mentioned bringing a cartoon to pass around at staff meetings to help them begin their work with a smile.

I am remembering one staff member in particular, Richard—Dick—Fears. The most prominent aspect of Dick's playfulness was his love of puns. He certainly would have bought into Oscar Levant's comment, "A pun is the lowest form of humor—when you don't think of it first." Though I knew better, I would sometimes try to improve on one of his puns, and I always lost. This would only stimulate his imagination to run wild, to our chorus of good natured groans. We had such good fun working together, even though it wasn't easy. We had very different work styles that we had to reconcile. In addition, we were living with increasingly difficult financial realities that eventually meant our partnership had to end too soon. In all those struggles our partnership, cemented with laughter, saw us through.

STEWARDSHIP, FUND RAISING, CHURCH BUDGETS

Once, when I was worshipping at a large African-American Church, the pastor announced a "Thank You Offering." He said, "If you have had a prayer answered, if God has blessed your life, if you are grateful, come and bring a gift to say, 'Thank you, God.'"

I was sitting on the platform, a courtesy this church afforded to visiting clergy, and so I had a good view of the proceedings. People jumped to their feet and streamed down the aisle with offerings in hand. The first people had given a gift even before an usher could put a plate in the minister's hands. Soon that plate was overflowing and had to be replaced by another. They were singing joyously, laughing and smiling as they came. Soon, I was also on my feet, joining the procession, grateful for this vital worship time, wanting to thank and to give.

Somehow, that is how it ought to be. Paul advised the Corinthians and us, "Each of you must give as you have made up your mind, not reluctantly or under compulsion, for God loves a *hilarious* giver." "Hilarious" is the literal translation of the Greek word there—*hilaron*—that is often tamely translated "cheerful." Paul goes on to promise, "And God is able to provide you with every blessing in abundance so that by always having

> **HUMOR IN THE CHURCH: THE RITE STUFF?**
>
> "Fight truth decay" is a favorite. "Come in for a free faith lift," is another—two examples of the toe-curling puns plastered across so many notice boards outside British churches.
>
> Now the hunt is on for the best pulpit pun, with a 500 pound ($985) prize for the number one religious slogan.
>
> "It never fails to amaze us how many interesting posters there are," said Margaret Slater of the church property specialists Congregational and General Insurance who are organizing the competition.
>
> "Some of the puns really make you smile and we've seen some great examples of creative copywriting too," she added.
>
> Among the classics she cited were, "Chxxch—Have you guessed what's missing? UR!" and "God, you're great!"
>
> (Reuters, Friday, March 23, 2007.

enough of everything, you may share abundantly in every good work." (2 Cor 9:7–8, NRSV, except for the word "hilarious.")

The teaching is clear. God's call to us to give is part of God's grace for us. In giving, we have opportunity not only to say thank you to God, but to enter into God's redemptive work in the world. We humans are hungry for meaning and purpose in our lives. God gives us an opportunity to express part of that meaning and purpose in one way each time there is an invitation to give. As such, the offering is the climax of worship. People can respond to God's call they heard in worship that day. Seen this way, the practice of humor in giving should be clearly evident—people should bring offerings smiling with thanksgiving and laughing with joy at such a privilege.

But that is not the way many people experience it. Rather for some, Sunday offering time and annual pledge campaigns stir resistance, guilt, and perhaps even resentment. There may be recriminations about grandiose plans, worries about one's own finances and employment as well as rising church expenses, and demands to see the "bottom line."

As Burton Howe notes, "If there is a subject that causes people in church to feel 'ill at ease,' it is the subject of stewardship. Humor breaks the ice and makes a serious point without putting people off." To this end, one church uses lighthearted skits to catch attention, stimulate thinking, and create interest. Another pastor speaks of telling a true life funny story at offertory time, a story that is related to trusting God for our needs, or experiencing the goodness of God.

Heather Entrekin has invited people to try tithing for a month as an experiment. She and her church have tried to create lightness and fun around the teaching of tithing. One year, they used the play on words, "Appetither"—Be one, eat one. As part of the festive atmosphere, they did serve appetizers at fellowship hour following worship. The next year, the theme was "Blest be the TITHE that binds." She notes, "It does get people's attention and, I think, helps create an openness that minimizes or reduces the anxiety often felt about the subject of stewardship."

BOARD MEETINGS

When I responded to my call to ministry as a young person, there was much that excited me. This included having the Bible and its truths come alive for me and others, the joy of leading worship and preaching, the privilege of being present to people when they hurt or grieved, and helping achieve important causes. I did not once think about going to church board meetings.

However, once I began my pastorates, I attended many board meetings, or as I too often referred to them "bored" meetings. At first, I was so busy learning the ropes that I didn't notice that many laypersons felt the same way. Recruitment was difficult, attendance low, recidivism high.

And not just in my church. In the mid nineties, Presbyterian Research Services conducted a survey of 605 elders (the major board in those churches) who were just coming off their three-year term of office. In response to a question about what surprised them in serving on their church board, 155 offered positive responses, while 199 gave negative responses. Twenty-nine percent reported they were weary and burned out.[2]

It was discovered that people agreed to go on their church's board with two expectations: that they had gifts that would be well-used by this board; and that they would grow spiritually while serving. Too often, neither of these hopes was satisfied. They left their board experience less enthused for their church than when they went in.

In the light of this need, Charles Olsen and Ellen Morseth worked with churches to create a more redemptive way of board life—a strikingly different "board culture." In time they called this new way, "Worshipful Work." Chuck Olsen wrote, "Spirituality has touched worship, education, counseling, and evangelism. It is now ready to touch administration."[3]

The transforming board culture they identified had four distinctive practices:

- History-giving and storytelling,
- Biblical / theological reflection—including story-weaving the church's story with a biblical story,
- Prayerful discernment, and
- Visioning the future.

I commend their writings and discoveries to all who seek a more meaningful board life.[4] While the entire process is beyond our scope, the first practice is very much related to our topic.

2. Reported by Olsen, *Transforming Church Boards*, 8.

3. Ibid., xvii.

4. In addition to *Transforming Church Boards*, I commend Morris and Olsen,

We have repeatedly noted that story is the bedrock of comedy and humor. Vital story engages the humor even if it is expressed simply in a relaxed face and body and twinkle of the eye and a little more trust in the group. Likewise, story is equally important for a board to know who they are and what the significance of the congregation they serve is. Olsen notes, "Whenever community and identity are threatened or lost, the way back is through story."[5]

A board needs to know, who is this church? What vision inspired its founding and what missions have animated its life? When did God seem closest? When was the blessing of God upon the church most clearly experienced?

In order to do this, stories must be told that reflect the church's "thick history." That is, what are the church's "defining moments?" Olsen reflects, "Thick history will reveal the lay people who have been influential in the life of the congregation—the people who embody the vision and character of the church. They make up the great 'cloud of witnesses' whose voices continue to be heard."[6]

"Thick history" also includes more recent events, such as what are the beautiful, creative, and redemptive moments each board member has experienced in the life of this church? How has God been at work in our church in the last month?

Olsen and Morseth suggest a shared storytelling. One person tells a small piece of a story of the church. Others can jump in at any time with "But before that . . ." or "And then . . ." or "Meanwhile, at the same time . . ."

I can assure you—when the story of a church's "thick history" flows, humor soon follows. There is play and delight and laughter, along with discovery and renewal. At the same time, though this is an effective process, it is not an "efficient" one if one is watching the clock. It takes time.

Board meetings may need to be restructured. Perhaps board retreats will be times when extensive exploration of story and thick history can take place. Still, honest sharing about God's discerned ways among us is brought by the humorous gift of story telling in the board meeting. It is well worth the time it takes to hear and/or tell a story!

Discerning God's Will Together; Morseth, *Ritual and the Arts in Spiritual Discernment*, Olsen and Morseth *Selecting Church Leaders*.

5. Olsen, *Transforming Church Boards*, 55.

6. Ibid., 58.

MORE CHURCH SIGNS:

(openers)
Come in and get your faith lifted.
Life is fragile; handle with prayer.
When in doubt, faith it.
Please come in and do an about faith.
First come, first saved.
Honk if you love Jesus. Text while driving if you want to meet Him.
(attendance encouragers)
Visitors welcome . . . members expected.
Trespassers welcome
We are open between Easter and Christmas
Stop here for your holiday spirits.
All new sermons—no summer reruns.
We reserve the right to accept everybody.
Our auditorium is prayer conditioned.
(At a church under repair)
Renovating going on inside. How about you?
(a holiday greeting)
Merry Christmas to our Christian friends. Happy Hanukkah to our Jewish friends. And to our atheist friends, Good Luck!

Controversy, Conflict, and Criticism

As clergy give leadership within a congregation and as they take stands and become involved in the issues facing community, society, and nation, there will be controversy. Where there is controversy, conflict will be present. And, almost certainly there will be criticism of the visible leader.

Bob Overstreet remembers such a time. Some years ago, while preaching a "Peace Sunday" sermon, he recalls, "I made fun of the Pentagon and its evacuation plan following an atomic blast to fly military personnel to bomb shelters in West Virginia where they would be safe underground. I ridiculed the military establishment, and I laughed as I described these soldiers fleeing to their bunkers to save the world. Others also laughed at my ludicrous picture, BUT one couple got up and walked out of the service. (I've never had that happen to me before or since!)

"Well, I patched it up; they remained members and I was able to minister to them my remaining years as their pastor. I had to visit them (a retired military officer and wife with a son who was a graduate of West Point serving overseas) explaining that my dad was a military chaplain and that I was formerly an army reserve chaplain. I explained that I was not demeaning persons who served their country, but I was attacking the philosophy that military might will save us from the evil in the world. I even invited the couple to write a 'counter' article in the church newsletter."

Bob reflects on what he learned from this, "Humility, for one thing—and that humor in the pulpit needs to be carefully crafted." He reflects further, "I think I was enjoying the laughs so much that I forgot to make my *real* point clear." In retrospect, he offers a self-criticism that his perhaps insensitive humor hit someone's raw nerve and necessitated a confrontation and conversation.

That may be, but there is something more. There is increasing peril that these tensions and conflicts will happen. From years in comedy, Bob Newhart notes, ". . . audiences have changed, too. We have lost our ability to laugh at ourselves."

Newhart goes on, "I don't have a joke on albino cross-dressers, but if I did, I guarantee you that I would receive a letter from the local chapter of the ACD asking me to cease and desist making fun of albino cross-dressers . . .

"The problem is that we live in an uptight country. Why don't we just laugh at ourselves? We are funny. Gays are funny. Straights are funny. Women are funny. Men are funny. We are all funny, and we all do funny things. Let's laugh about it."[7]

Sadly these days, this brittleness Newhart notes, this touchiness, this inability to play, joke, and tease about our differences seems most evident among religious people. In her beautiful but sad memoir, *Leaving Church*, Barbara Brown Taylor tells of why she had to resign from being priest to a parish that she deeply loved.

There were several factors she mentions. A significant one was that a "hardening" was taking place in church life. There were growing debates and contentiousness over biblical literalism, particularly in regard to the

7. Newhart, *I Shouldn't Even Be Doing This!*, 174.

place of gay and lesbian people in the church. She found people succumbing to the temptation of which Arun Gandhi spoke, "People of the Book risk putting the book above people." She said that she and others "began to mistake the words on a page for the realities they describe . . . to love the dried ink marks on the page more than . . . the encounters that gave rise to them." As a result of these debates, she wrote, "the poets began drifting away from churches as the jurists grew louder and more insistent."[8]

This, along with other pressures and disappointments, was proving toxic to her own love relationship with God. And so, when the president of nearby Piedmont College offered her a job teaching basic religion courses to young adults, she immediately accepted, resigned her pastorate, and quickly left.

While each of us must follow our own leading, are there other ways for us church leaders to respond to the criticism, conflict, and controversy that will swirl around us from time to time? Is a practice of humor of any help in this quagmire? Can the practice of humor be summoned even while so much of our world seems to be losing its sense of humor? If so, this may be the greatest gift of humor to ministry we have yet discovered. Consider an example from history.

Interlude—lessons from Abraham Lincoln

Among his other contributions, Abraham Lincoln is remembered as the greatest storyteller and humorist among American presidents. He certainly used his humor in his life of competition, elections, and debates. Nor did his humor forsake him as he faced terrible conflicts, harsh criticism, and name calling. There may well be lessons to learn from him as to how humor can help us navigate these waters.

At the same time, Benjamin Thomas has offered some cautions to those of us approaching Lincoln's humor. For one thing, it is hard to discern which of "Lincoln's stories" he actually told. Many a good story attributed to him, may well be from another source. For another, his humor is of his age, merging pioneer exaggeration and earthiness with Yankee laconic minimalism. And again, we will miss much because of the great skill of the original storyteller. Lincoln, it is said, was a master of mimicry and many dialects. His enthusiasm for a story and the joy

8. Taylor, *Leaving Church*, The quotes are from 106, 107, 111.

of telling it would carry the day with sometimes rather commonplace humor.[9] Even with these cautions, there is much to consider.

In the course of his life, he was subjected to much abuse and name calling. As Alex Ayers notes, he was called a baboon, a buffoon, an ape, a clown, a tyrant, a usurper, a monster, an idiot, a eunuch, a demagogue, an atheist, a blunderer, a bully, a Judas Iscariot, a Nero, a charlatan, a joker, and an ugly fool.[10]

How did Lincoln respond to this barrage of name calling? For one thing, with a good bit of self-humor. When, in a debate, Stephen Douglas accused him of being two-faced, Lincoln responded, "I leave it to you, my friends. If I had two faces would I be wearing this one?"[11] He so often joked about his own appearance that he may have been capitalizing on his homeliness. Another of his stories had to do with an ugly man on a narrow road who met a woman. The woman said, "Well, you are the ugliest man I ever saw." "Perhaps so, he admitted, but I can't help that madam." She responded, "No, I suppose not, but you might stay at home."[12]

This self-humor enabled him to keep working with some rather testy cabinet members. Once, he sent a delegation to Secretary of War Stanton with orders to grant their request. They returned to say Stanton had not only refused, but had called Lincoln a fool for sending such an order. With mock astonishment, Lincoln responded, "Did Stanton call me a fool? Well I guess I'd better go over and see Stanton about this. Stanton is usually right."[13]

On another occasion, a friend expressed concern that cabinet member Salmon P. Chase was ambitious for the presidency. Lincoln responded that Chase's department was functioning very well, and as long as it did so, he wouldn't worry about Chase's aspirations. It reminded him of a time when he and his stepbrother were plowing a cornfield in Indiana. Lincoln was driving the horse, his stepbrother guiding the plow. The horse was lazy and slow but then suddenly rushed across the field so fast they could hardly keep up. On reaching the furrow's end, Lincoln found an enormous chin fly biting the horse and knocked it off. His step brother objected, "That's all that made him go." Lincoln concluded,

9. Thomas, *"Lincoln's Humor"and OtherEssays*, 3–5.

10. Ayers, *The Wit and Wisdom of Abraham Lincoln*, 151–52.

11. Ibid., 186.

12. Thomas, "*Lincoln's Humor*," 12.

13. Ibid.

"Now if Mr. Chase has a presidential chin fly biting him, I'm not going to knock it off if it will only make his department go."[14]

At times he would turn the humor on the other. In one of their debates, Stephen Douglas tried to score a point by recalling Lincoln was once a lowly storekeeper, selling among other things whiskey and cigars, and "Mr. Lincoln was a very good bartender!" Lincoln acknowledged the truth of that and added that in those days, Douglas was one of his best customers. He added, "The difference between us now is this: I have left my side of the counter, but Mr. Douglas still sticks to his as tenaciously as ever."

On another occasion, Lincoln attended a service conducted by Rev. Peter Cartwright, against whom he was running for congress. In his sermon, Cartwright asked those who wanted to go to heaven to stand. Then he asked all those who did not want to go to hell to stand. Lincoln was the only one not to stand either time. Cartwright then called upon Lincoln to say where he was going. Lincoln responded, "I am going to Congress."[15] And he did, he won the election.

He well understood the nature of conflict, and at times, his humor revealed this. He once described a battle between his sons Willie and Tad that what was wrong with them was ". . . just what's the matter with the whole world. I've got three walnuts and each wants two." Though he had to preside over the bloody Civil War, at an earlier time, he strongly opposed the Mexican War, noting "Young America is very anxious to fight for the liberation of enslaved nations and colonies, provided always, that they have land." He noted that even the town loafer was stirred up with patriotism for the war. Lincoln reported that the old guy told him, "I feel patriotic." When Lincoln queried what he meant by that, the "old geezer" responded, "Why, when I get this way, I feel like I want to kill somebody or steal something."[16]

It was once his duty to deliver an official reprimand to a young officer who had been court-martialed. His offense was quarreling with an officer of a higher rank. After pointing to the futility of quarreling both with those above and below one, he wrote, "Better give your path to a dog than be bitten by him in contesting for the right. Even killing

14. Ibid., 6–7.

15. Ayers, *The Wit and Wisdom*, 23, 43.

16. Ibid., 129.

the dog would not cure the bite."[17] In another disciplinary responsibility, he resisted applying the death penalty to soldiers who deserted because of cowardice, because, as he said, "It would frighten the poor devils to death to shoot them."[18]

Lincoln employed humor for many reasons. For one thing, it was a way of getting on good terms with people. Other times, humor softened his own pain and frustration. When he lost the 1858 Senate race, he commented, "I feel somewhat like the boy in Kentucky who stubbed his toe while running to see his sweetheart. The boy said he was too big to cry, and felt far too badly hurt to laugh."[19]

Further, he used humor to escape a difficult position or to avoid making an embarrassing commitment. (Once, when forced to listen to a long reading on spiritualism, when asked what he thought of it, responded, "Well, for those who like that sort of thing I should think that is just about the sort of thing they would like.")[20]

And again, his humor softened many a refusal of a privilege or appointment or rebuke that he had to deliver. (When diagnosed with a contagious, but mild small pox, he observed, "There's one good thing about this. I now have something I can give everybody.")[21]

Above all of these, his most frequent use of his wit was as an aid to clarity or meaning. His conversation and his writing were freighted with story, simile, and metaphor. These assured that meaning was not only clearly communicated, but long remembered.[22]

He also found in humor a needed safety valve for his overburdened mind. Indeed, humor was often interspersed with his heavy and tragic responsibilities. On September 21, 1862, he called his cabinet together for a special meeting. He was reading a book when they arrived. Then he asked if they had ever read anything by the great humorist Artemus Ward. He then read them a sketch titled, "A High Handed Outrage at Utica," and laughed heartily, though no one else joined in. Stanton was so outraged that he almost walked out.

17. Ibid., 172, 158–9.

18. Thomas, "*Lincoln's Humor*," 9.

19. Ayers, *The Wit and Wisdom*, 55.

20. Ibid., 182.

21. Ibid., 176–77.

22. These uses Lincoln put to humor are listed and described in Thomas, "*Lincoln's Humor*," 14–15.

Then Lincoln asked, "Why don't you laugh? With the fearful strain that is upon me night and day, if I did not laugh I should die, and you need this medicine as much as I do."

He then reached into his tall hat, which he had placed on the table and pulled out a paper. He told the cabinet that he had prepared a little paper of much significance—the fulfillment of a promise he had made to his Maker. With firm voice, he read to them the announcement of the Emancipation Proclamation: "On the first day of January in the year of our Lord, one thousand eight hundred and sixty-three, all persons held as slaves . . . shall be then, thenceforward, and forever free."

The formerly irritated cabinet was now stunned. Stanton later noted "If reading a chapter of Artemus Ward is a prelude to such a deed as this, the book should be filed among the archives of the nation and the author canonized."[23]

Back to the twenty-first century

How does humor help us deal with conflict and criticism? When I told my friend Ron, a retired minister, I was exploring humor as a practice to lend perspective for ministry, he had an immediate response. "I think you're on to something," he said. "When I was in the pastorate, I took myself far too seriously."

Perhaps this is the place to start. We can learn from Lincoln, not to take ourselves too seriously. We need to realize that each time one of our suggestions to a board / church is ignored or turned down—until someone else proposes it—that often goes with being a leader. It may be equally important to realize that attacks that seem personal are on the position we occupy, the institution we represent, or the stance we hold on an issue. And even when the attack is very personal, it's possible to realize that's not very important.

Self-humor and playfulness can help one survive and perhaps even thrive in the midst of criticism. At least, one is being noticed! Tend to, care for, and keep a perspective on self.

Further, humor of all sorts can contribute to one's resilience and inner strength in the face of pressure and can soften life's hurts. Lincoln was subject to times of much sadness, melancholy, and depression. Quite clearly his love of story and humor was part of his way of bouncing back from painful experiences.

23. Ayers, *The Wit and Wisdom*, 68–69.

THE FUN OF CHURCH NEWSLETTER AND BULLETIN BLOOPERS

The cost for attending the Fasting and Prayer conference includes meals.

Our youth basketball team is back in action Wednesday at 8 p.m. in the recreation hall. Come out and watch us kill "Christ the King".

The peacemaking meeting scheduled for today has been canceled due to a conflict.

The sermon this morning is "Jesus Walks on the Water." The sermon tonight will be "Searching for Jesus."

Next Thursday there will be tryouts for the choir. They need all the help they can get.

Eight new choir robes are currently needed due to the addition of several new members and to the deterioration of some older ones.

Bertha Belch, a missionary from Africa will be speaking tonight at Calvary Memorial Church. Come and hear Bertha Belch all the way from Africa.

Potluck supper Sunday at 5 p.m. Prayer and medication to follow.

The Low Self Esteem Support Group will meet Thursday at 7 p.m. Please use the back door.

Weight Watchers will meet at 7 p.m. at the First Presbyterian Church. Please use the large double door at the side entrance.

The anthem by the choir will be "Sin and Rejoice" by Johann Sebastian Bich.

Before walking further into this, there are some cautions to consider. In their wise and sensitive book, *Crucial Conversations: Tools for Talking When Stakes Are High,* Kerry Patterson and associates only speak of jokes / humor once. In a "style under stress" inventory, one of the items to check true or false is, "Rather than tell people exactly what I think, sometimes I rely on jokes . . . to let them know I'm frustrated." The scoring key reveals this as a "masking mechanism."[24] That's all they say about humor, preferring a more straightforward approach. Other

24. Patterson, Grenny, McMillan, and Switzler, *Crucial Conversations*, 57, 61.

psychologists and counselors have noted that humor can be a defense mechanism. If not a masking device, perhaps humor is sometimes an avoiding device. It is wise to recognize that humor can be used to ignore, deny, avert, or mask a conflict that needs to happen. It is also wise to resolve, that as much as one is aware, not to do this.

There is another side to this, however. Sometimes a conflict does not need to be engaged at the moment it is raised. Perhaps it should not be. Humor may be one way to delay the onset of the conflict discussion until a better time. Also humor may contribute to relaxing the atmosphere maybe even inviting a friendly confrontation so that it can be more constructively carried on.

One other caution needs to be mentioned. We have earlier spoken of satire and sarcasm as mostly humor to hurt. As long as there is hope of resolving or transforming the conflict so that there is constructive gain in relationship, these "weapons of humor" should be set aside.

In addition to increasing one's self perspective and resilience, humor can make many contributions to situations of conflict. For one thing, it can open doors so that where there was only silence before, now something can be discussed. Allen Klein tells a story, not of conflict, but of another unspoken issue. A woman named Laura who had ovarian cancer had prepared a meal for people she cared about. She relates, "I stepped into the bathroom, looked in the mirror and gasped! The entire front of my wig was a solid melted glob of plastic fibers. (Obviously I had gotten too close to the oven when I was basting the bird.) What I couldn't believe was that NO ONE had said a word. They were trying to spare me the embarrassment.

"I walked back into the dining room laughing so hard at the thought of all of them trying to ignore the hilarious sight of me in that wig. The laughter was contagious . . . and led us into the first heart-to-heart conversation we had had since my diagnosis. The shields went down and hearts connected."[25]

Humor can also blunt or defuse sensitive or volatile issues. When President Reagan, in the midst of one of the debates was queried about his advanced age, he responded, "I will not make age an issue of this campaign. I am not going to exploit, for political purposes, my opponent's youth and inexperience." On another occasion, he responded to derogatory comments about his age, "Andrew Jackson was seventy-five years

25. Klein, *The Courage to Laugh*, 50.

old and still vigorous when he left the White House. I know because he told me."[26] Humorously and playfully, President Reagan communicated important points in this issue, that there are two sides to it, and age has its advantages as well. Having established that, the debate could move on to more substantive topics.

Humor can also help one avoid unnecessary issues or confrontations. The eighteenth-century philosopher Moses Mendelssohn was walking down a street in Berlin one day when he accidentally collided with a stout Prussian officer. "Swine!" bellowed the officer. Rather than risk physical abuse by responding in kind, he instead tipped his hat, gave the officer a low courteous bow and replied, "Mendelssohn."[27]

Further, humor can sometimes help the conflicting parties get beyond their impasse. It is said that during the Cuban missile crisis, Soviet and American negotiators became deadlocked. They sat in silence until someone suggested that each person tell a joke or humorous story. One of the Russians offered this riddle, "What is the difference between capitalism and communism?" He then provided the answer, "In capitalism man exploits man. In communism, it's the other way around." With the mood somewhat relaxed, they kept talking and catastrophic confrontation was avoided.[28]

In chapter six, when we spoke of humor and pastoral care, we spoke of humor's role in "reframing" an individual's problem or issue. Perhaps the same thing can happen when the people of God are in conflict. With inner strength, joy, and resilience, humor may help open doors, defuse explosive situations, and break impasses. Then, perhaps something more will happen.

We—all of us, all sides—will begin to reframe this. We will see our confrontation in a whole new perspective. We may discover that great wisdom is to be found in a wider range of views. Or we may come to see the differences are not as great, or important, or hopeless as we had feared. We may come to like and enjoy some on "the other side."

The reframing may include a view from God's perspective of God's beloved creatures both missing and finding great truths about the One they hope to serve. Such transformation in conflict has happened before, and it can happen again.

26. Quoted in Klein, *The Healing Power of Humor*, 50.

27. Ibid., 5.

28. Ibid., 9.

QUESTIONS FOR PERSONAL AND GROUP REFLECTION

1. Where, if anywhere, has humor enhanced or lightened your tasks of administrative leadership?
2. In what ways, if any, has humor and story enriched board meetings and other leadership activities of the churches where you have participated or served?
3. What, if any, gifts of humor do you and your fellow staff members use in your life and work together?
4. When, if ever, has humor been helpful in the fundraising and other stewardship efforts of congregations where you were a part?
5. What insights, discoveries, and patterns would you like to take from Abraham Lincoln as regards criticism and conflict?
6. Have you ever employed humor during a conflict? What was your experience?
7. Have you ever used humor when being criticized (during or after the time of the criticism)? What reflections do you have about that?
8. Are there other areas of administration, not mentioned in this chapter, where you found humor helpful?
9. What are you learning about the practice of humor as a resource for you personally and for your ministry?

9

How Do You Get There from Here?

(Identifying and Developing a New Spiritual Practice)

Anyone who calls himself or herself 'Christian'
and is without a sense of humor may well be taking the name in vain.

—Doris Donnelly[1]

Friedrich Nietzsche once said that the Christians would need to sing better songs before he would believe in their redeemer.

—Charles Marsh[2]

I enjoy the New England type of humor. In one of my favorites, a stranger traveling in Maine stops and asks a wizened resident for directions to a certain place. The old timer starts, giving over-detailed instruction (a trademark of such stories) but then decides that won't work. He starts again and again, but finally concludes, "I don't think you can get there from here."

Can we get there from here? That's actually two questions. One is this—since humor is has been so helpful for me as a spiritual practice, how can I now convince you to believe that it is indeed a spiritual practice worthy of your acceptance? Two, if you are convinced but don't know what to do about it, how do you develop this practice? How do we get there from here?

1. Donnelly, "Divine Folly," 395.
2. Marsh, "From the Phraseological to the Real."

DISCIPLINE AND PRACTICE

Before those two questions, however, there is a preliminary one—what specifically do I mean, humor as a spiritual practice? Actually, we need clearer, more detailed definitions of two terms, practice and discipline.

Practice

"Practice" can simply mean what we do, or it can mean to work at something in order to improve.

But it also has a deeper and more specific meaning. It is the term that Craig Dykstra, Dorothy Bass, and those in the Practicing Our Faith project at Valparaiso University selected and redefined for an important perspective.

Bass begins the book she edited on this subject by recalling a family spiritual retreat and longing for ways to keep alive the moral / spiritual guidance and support her family experienced at that time.[3]

A team of Christian leaders has worked together to reflect, discover, and in turn, offer a richer and deeper grasping of what it means to live as Christians in such times of great change as Bass's family was experiencing.

The key concept in their approach is that of *practices.* "Practices are those shared activities that address fundamental human needs and that, woven together, form a way of life."[4] They are offered to lead to encounters with God in faithful living that change lives.

These practices arise from listening to the wisdom of the Christian tradition and those who can guide us in living it. This is done in company with other believers / searchers, some from around our contemporary world and others from the many centuries before us, the "communion of saints."

Dykstra and Bass further enlarge on this definition, "*Christian practices are things Christian people do together over time in response to and in the light of God's active presence for the life of the world . . .*"[5] These are ordinary activities, things people may do every day. There is additional power when a combination of such practices are discovered and woven together.

3. Bass, *Practicing Our Faith*, x.

4. Ibid., xi.

5. Ibid., 5, italics theirs.

Even more, these practices may "create openings in our lives where the grace, mercy, and presence of God may be made known to us . . ."[6]

The practices, thus chosen, are interrelated and flow into one another. Starting with just one may well lead a person on to the practice of yet others, and indeed into them all. These are practices that our world needs, and they are also practices that are in trouble in today's world.

They offer this concise summary, "Each practice

- Involves us in God's activities in the world and reflects God's grace and love
- Is a complex set of acts, words, and images that addresses one area of fundamental human need
- Is learned with and from other people
- Comes to us from the past and will be shaped by us for the future
- Is thought-full; it implies certain beliefs about ourselves, our neighbors, and God
- Is done within the church, in the public realm, in daily work, and at home
- Shapes the people who participate in the practice, individually and communally
- Has good purposes, although it often becomes corrupted
- Comes to a focus in worship."[7]

This group of scholars selected these twelve practices: honoring the body; hospitality; household economics; saying yes and saying no; keeping Sabbath; testimony; discernment; shaping communities; forgiveness; healing; dying well; and singing our lives. Though these are both individual and communal, the emphasis seems to be on the communal aspects.

Discipline

Before they developed this concept, a widespread term to describe committed exploration / acts into Christian growth was "discipline." This term is closely related to "disciple" meaning student, follower, or devotee. The road to deeper discipleship involves disciplines of the spirit and

6. http://www.practicingourfaith.com; "What are Christian Practices?"
7. Ibid.

has been described by many writers. One of the most influential and well-known developments of this theme is *Celebration of Discipline* by Richard Foster.

In the introduction of this book, Foster tells of how he came to write the book. Many factors came together including his own sense of spiritual bankruptcy early in his ministry, the needy people with whom he ministered, and the witness / mentoring of several vital Christian leaders.

Out of this, he identified twelve disciplines necessary for Christian growth and wrote a chapter about each. He spoke of inward disciplines (meditation, prayer, fasting, study); outward disciplines (simplicity, solitude, submission, service); and corporate disciplines (confession, worship, guidance, celebration). While his list is also individual and communal, the emphasis seems to be more on the individual. His book has long touched a widespread hunger. It is still being helpfully read by many people, some thirty years after it was written.

Comparison and contrast

It is fascinating to put these two—Foster's chosen disciplines and Bass and associates' selection of practices side by side and compare them. (I have placed words from the two lists side by side when they appear to be the same or similar.)

Richard Foster—Disciplines	Dorothy Bass (et al)—Practices
INWARD	
1. Meditation	
2. Prayer	
3. Fasting	
4. Study	
OUTWARD	
5. Simplicity	Household economics
6. Solitude	
7. Submission	
8. Service	
CORPORATE	
9. Confession	
10. Worship	Keeping Sabbath

Richard Foster—Disciplines	Dorothy Bass (et al)—Practices
11. Guidance	Discernment
12. Celebration	Singing our lifes
	Honoring the body
	Hospitality
	Saying yes and saying no
	Testimony
	Shaping Communities
	Forgiveness
	Healing
	Dying well

These lists are not as different as first might appear. Some on the other list is assumed by each. For example, Bass says that Bible study and prayer are assumed in each of the practices. However, when I listed these disciplines / practices side-by-side, they do not speak of exactly the same thing, either. Each has emphasis and nuance of its own. Together, discipline and practice offer an impressive array of invitations to spiritual growth and steps to move in that direction.

About lists and numbers

Each of these two approaches lists twelve disciplines / practices. But is twelve a sacred number? Should there be no more and no less than that in laying out a path of Christian growth? I raised that question, and Don Richter, of the Practicing Our Faith project, responded "There is no definitive set of twelve Christian practices."[8] He said the co-authors of *Practicing Our Faith* considered a much longer list but settled on these as most compelling. This meant that some worthy possibilities needed to be combined into broader entities.

Richter pointed out further that a variety of factors might mean that the list of practices would need to change or expand.

- The change might be due to the age of the persons doing the practices. For example, when this organization undertook a book (and website) on spiritual practices for teens (with a teenager as co-author of each chapter), some of the original list remained, but it expanded to include items closer to where teens live their lives.

8. Don Richter, personal email, 4/17/2008.

Eighteen practices were chosen that included youthful concerns of creativity, work, play, and truth.[9]

- And when they went on to offer guidance on spiritual practices for emerging adults in their 20s, again, some of the original list was included, but practices addressing life concerns of persons in that age span were considered. Among these were study, friendship and intimacy, discerning God's will, knowing / loving our neighbors of other faiths, and peacemaking / nonviolence.[10]
- Or the list of practices might need to be adapted to fit the particular culture and customs in which it is formulated. For example, a group of Korean-American theologians suggested the practice of "ricing" as the form of Christian hospitality that would be germane to their cultural setting.[11]
- A rural church in North Carolina is experiencing renewal through the practice of gardening.
- And so we see that Christian practices may be tailored to fit specific needs such as life stage, life situation, culture, and economic setting. Certainly, practices might also be selected to address the special situation of persons in a given occupation / calling, and / or living with particular stressors.

This is where my suggestion of humor as spiritual practice deserves consideration. In these days, many church leaders are living with great criticism, conflict, strain, and job uncertainty. There is temptation toward ineffectiveness due to depression and pain. Many are considering "dropping out" and some do!

Therefore, I submit that humor as a spiritual practice is much needed for church leaders particularly at this juncture of history. Of course, they are not alone in this. Humor as a spiritual practice has widespread possibility for all.

I have demonstrated that humor consistently practiced brings many gifts to Christian living and to ministry. It includes these:

- Hope/hopefulness when contending with depression and despair,
- Perspective on problems or topics that may seem daunting and overwhelming,

9. Bass and Richter, *Way to Live.*

10. Bass and Briehl, *On Our Way.*

11. Pak, Lee, Kim, and Cho, *Singing the Lord's Song in a New Land.*

- Balance in priority and in concepts,
- Breathing space and respite in conflict and criticism,
- Softening of the lines in conflict, and perhaps steps toward reconciliation or at least toward civility,
- An invitation to the possibility of forgiveness,
- A reactivating of joy in faith, in service, and in ministry.[12]

But is humor a spiritual practice?

I had an "ah ha" moment on this question when reading Barbara Brown Taylor's book *An Altar in the World*. She explores a variety of Christian practices, some well-accepted, some not usually on such lists. Included is a chapter on wilderness and getting lost, recalling the first time her husband Ed and she went to Mexico. They were lost most of the time, met people willing to help, and saw things they would not otherwise have seen.

Then she writes, "I know it is a stretch to call this a spiritual practice, but perhaps that is the point. *Anything can become a spiritual practice once you are willing to approach it that way*—once you let it bring you to your knees and show you what is real, including who you really are, who other people are, and how near God can be when you have lost your way."[13] For her, getting lost was one of her "altars in the world," and she explores a fascinating array of such altars, although humor is not one of her explicit choices.

> "In life, the only two tools you need are WD40 and duct tape. That is because all of life's problems break down into one of two categories: something moves and it shouldn't, or it doesn't move and it should . . . Humor is the WD40 and the duct tape of life. Like WD 40 on those rusted clips, humor jars us loose, breaks us open, and makes us see things in a fresh new way. And like the duct tape on the pack, it bonds us together by highlighting our commonalities." (Susan Sparks, *Laugh Your Way to Grace*, 65.)

12. For a slightly different perspective on humor's benefits, see chapter 4, "Happiness Attracts," in Martin, S. J., *Between Heaven and Mirth* where he offers, "11½ Serious Reasons for Good Humor," 86–119.

13. Taylor, *An Altar in the World*, 82–83. Italics are added.

I suggest we add humor to our "altars in the world", our spiritual practices. Recall some of our witnesses:

- Peter Berger spoke of comic laughter as "transcendence in a lower key" and "redeeming laughter," healing in the present and sign of God's greater surprises to come.[14]
- Conrad Hyers commented, ". . . though joy and humor are certainly not synonymous, neither are they alien. Humor is not displaced by joy but is one of its forms of expression."[15]
- Victor Frankl on his experience in the Nazi concentration camp, "Humor was another of the soul's weapons in the fight for self-preservation . . . [humor] can afford an aloofness and an ability to rise above any situation."[16]

To employ the descriptors that the spiritual practices leaders use, these expressions of humor are "shared activities" that "address a fundamental human need" and can be "interwoven with other practices to form a way of life." As with other practices, we learn it from our heritage—at least some voices within it—from biblical times on. Laughter, clapping, singing and rejoicing are indeed things people do "in response to and in the light of God's active presence for the life of the world."

Good humor and play "are ordinary activities, the stuff of everyday life" and "can be shaped in response to God's active presence." Joyful laughter may indeed "create openings in our lives where grace, mercy, and presence of God may be known to us"—or an expression that this has been recognized and claimed.

Humor can be interwoven with the practices of keeping Sabbath, singing our lives, hospitality, shaping communities, and dying well, among others.

Conrad Hyers once noted, "It was a most unfortunate omission on the part of medieval Christianity not to have included humor and humorlessness in its moral glossary of the seven cardinal virtues and the seven deadly sins."[17]

14. Berger, *Redeeming Laughter*, 205.
15. Hyers, *Holy Laughter*, 239.
16. Frankl, *Man's Search for Meaning*, 68–69.
17. Hyers, *Holy Laughter*, 227.

Joyful / hopeful laughter is a basic Christian practice that deserves to be cultivated and strengthened in mutual enrichment with the other practices.

Richter suggests an alternative way of viewing this. He writes, "Could it be that humor, like creativity, is a capacity that invigorates every Christian practice? Certainly the activity of forgiving and receiving forgiveness, for instance, has a different gestalt when appropriate humor is involved. Humor can disarm oneself and others, as together we acknowledge human foibles and finitude. Likewise hospitality infused with humor makes both host and guest feel welcome and at home."[18]

That is true, but at the same time it needs attention and development to do these things. And so I propose the intentional Christian practice of humor. Whether my chosen term appeals to you or not is not as important as seeing that self-care, and this kind of self-care in particular, is important for thriving in this calling.

What additional practices / disciplines are needed in ministry?

Church leaders share with all Christian believers the need to be attentive to the practices we have noted so far. At the same time, for us, certain practices need extra emphasis. In these brittle times among God's people, there is a call for resilient and resourceful pastoral leaders, persons who are sustained and renewed by God's care.

And so each person in ministry may need additional practices (or special emphasis on some) to equip one for one's particular leadership. The practice of *study* needs to be a constant. It may relate to one's particular responsibility, or it may relate to growth of one's spirit, new theological perspectives, or deeper understanding of contemporary issues and eras. The practice of study is so needed (and so obvious when it is absent).

Also, many a church leader will have responsibility in an institution and building with aging infrastructure in a time of declining financial resources. These facts will also impact their own salaries and job security. The practices of "*household economics*" and "*saying yes and saying no*" and the discipline of "*simplicity*" may need to be developed to a new

18. Richter, personal email, 4/17/2008.

level so it will call forth the creativity, imagination, and trustfulness needed in stewardship leadership through such a labyrinth.

And again, surveys also repeatedly discover that many clergy are lonely people. L. Gregory Jones and Kevin R. Armstrong speak of the vital role of "*holy friendships*" in sustaining excellence in ministry. Their vision includes but goes beyond the one-on-one or group of ministers who have a great deal in common. (This book has been designed to be a resource for such relationship building groups, with discussion / activity questions at the end of each chapter.)

Jones and Armstrong suggest that holy friendship may be especially enriching when it is forged across many differences between people. Further, they challenge the old notion that pastors cannot be friends with persons in their own congregation. Pastoral confidences must always be kept, of course, but that should not stand in the way of deep love and mutual support as people live and work alongside each other.[19] Turning to a "spiritual friend" as guide and director for one's spiritual journey is also a wise decision.

The spiritual practices of "*hospitality*" and "*shaping communities*" may need to be probed in depth so that clergy find the "holy friendships," the support and human / divine solace needed for ministry in changing and often difficult times.

There also seems to be a good bit of depression among those leading churches. If stress is a contributor to depression, there are reasons aplenty for clergy depression.

Depression is a psychological / theological illness. It can be treated both with psychological resources and theological ones. Rest, exercise, good nutrition, perhaps medication, and talk therapy can help. Prayer, meditation, lament, and holy friendships are all part of means of healing.

And, humor helps, though humor by itself does not cure depression. However, in conjunction with the methods we just mentioned, it can be a great aid on the way to spiritual health. Self-humor and, perhaps, sometimes a little hostile humor on the way out of a time of depression are both part of the cure and a sign of recuperation.

19. Jones and Armstrong, *Resurrecting Excellence*, 60–61. These paragraphs on clergy are a brief sampling and summary of a much more extensive discussion, part of Duke University's major research project, *Pulpit & Pew* to investigate the state of Protestant and Catholic pastoral leadership in the U.S.

The laughter that Christian grace, hope, and joy make possible sustains us in ministry. Recognizing and celebrating humor is called for. We have been touched with a mighty love. It behooves us to respond with smiles, laughter, and shouts of joy. That is why I am convinced that humor is a vital and much needed spiritual practice.

HOW CAN WE GROW IN OUR PRACTICES OF HUMOR?

Give me a sense of humor, Lord. Give me the grace to see a joke, to get some happiness in life and pass it on to other folk.

—A verse on the wall of Chester Cathedral in England

I now move to the second "How do we get there from here?" question. If one is now convinced of humor's spiritual importance and helpfulness but feels paralyzed or unqualified—permanently or temporarily—in exercising it, what then?

(Reader Alert: the author of these suggestions is a member of the ethnic group described in John Louis Anderson's book, *Scandinavian Humor and Other Myths.* He sees this book as an extended hilarious description of the supposed humorlessness of Norwegians, Swedes, Danes, and Finns. Further, he is of Puritan heritage, and a child of the Midwest drought / depression era. The reader may conclude this author doesn't know what he's talking about. Or, the reader may decide that if with those genes he can attempt a little humor, there is hope for all. With that caution, we will let him proceed.)

Approach this section in the gentle spirit of a "brainstorm." Or better yet, to use a Scandinavian term, a "Smorgasbord." You can

> From the "Weird News" section of the newspaper
>
> "A 2006 Church of England report warned that disagreeable congregants, together with the pressures of the church's 'feudal system' bureaucracy, were turning priests harshly negative and creating an 'irritable clergy syndrome.' One of the report's authors told *The Times* of London in December that priests are bothered by 'having to be nice all the time to everyone, even when confronted with extremes of nastiness,' such as aggressive and neurotic parishioners." (from *Kansas City Star*, Feb 2, 2007, .F1.)

decide you want large portions of one or two selections, or a little of a lot of them.

Playfully consider the many suggestions, and add any others that come to mind. Don't take it too seriously and don't let it overwhelm or burden you. You don't have to eat it all, and you can always come back for seconds. You can "walk around the serving table" so to speak and then, come back and pick one or a few that appeal and may be truly helpful to you.

Begin with a theological perspective of humor

I hope to have convinced you that theologically, humor is fitting, needful, and called for. Recall Frederick Buechner's observation, ". . . only when we hear the gospel as a wild and marvelous joke [do we] really hear it at all . . . Heard as a joke—high and unbidden and ringing with laughter—it can only be God's thing."[20] This concurs so well with Paul's description of his/our being "fools for Christ's sake" (1 Cor 4:10).

We serve the One who offered this beatitude, "Blessed are you when people revile you and persecute you and utter all kinds of evil against you falsely on my account. *Rejoice and be glad*, for your reward is great in heaven, for in the same way they persecuted the prophets before you" (Matt 5:11–12, italics added).

We serve in a revolutionary counter-culture calling in which misunderstanding, criticism, and quite possibly more are to be expected. We do this with a message few will believe until they realize it is a joke—a wondrous divine joke. Then they join us in the laughter. Start from that perspective—that inviting humor is a God thing.

Recognize and appreciate others' humor

Even when convinced, some of us may feel we don't have much humor to offer. And so a next step is to recognize, appreciate, and enjoy the humor of others. Almost anyone would rather hear you laugh at his/her joke or prank than laugh at yours! That can be a quiet smile or a "laugh out loud" response. From time to time we have spoken of Annette Goodheart and her *Laughter Therapy*. The subtitle of her book is *How to Laugh About Everything in Your Life That Isn't Really Funny*. She teaches laughter as a healing practice. The laughter is taught and practiced in

20. Buechner, *Telling the Truth*, 68.

and of itself; without any jokes or humor to stimulate it. Her approach, now paralleled by the Laughing Yoga movement I mentioned in chapter 3 is well worth exploring. I will tell a bit more of Goodheart's approach later in this chapter.

If you happen to have a loud and ready laugh, you have a gift that can bring you close to many people. I hope that one of you is present in any gathering where I am going to tell or do something I hope is funny! Your laughter will stimulate laughter in others and will help them to relax and enjoy themselves.

Go deeper into story and become the story

Seek the bedrock of humor—story. But seek authentic story. Don't settle for cute little sermon illustrations found in the internet or in books that provide hundreds of them. Rather seek story in its truth and depth in your life, those of your family, and those with whom you minister and for whom you care. You may want to read biographies of people you admire.

Read gifted storytellers and observe how they discover and tell a story and learn from them. For example, on a blue day, Anne Lamott reluctantly accepted an invitation from a friend to go on a hike. Though stylishly dressed, they walked by / through a marsh that was wetter, muddier, and slipperier than they realized, and as they climbed a little bank, they fell down in the mud. These simple events stirred awareness and healing for Anne, and when she reflected on it and wrote it, it did the same for thousands of us. She called her story "Into Thin Mud." Read it both for what you receive and what you can learn about storytelling.[21]

As my teachers told me, "become the story." Find, ponder, reflect, and share stories that deeply connect to you. Then don't worry about whether there is any laughter when you tell it. Story carries itself and has a hidden gentle humor within.

Relax and do not force it

Sometimes I need to remind myself—and it may be helpful to you as well—to relax. Don't tense up, push, or overdo your humor for yourself or for others. And don't worry if people are not laughing at you or with you. If I can just take deep breaths and enjoy the people I am with,

21. Lamott, *Traveling Mercies*, 257–65.

people will have a good experience together. And (to repeat myself just once more) it is much more important for me to laugh than to make others laugh.

One of my rich little memories is of my mother doing this very thing. She sat across the table from me at a large family gathering and was quietly amused at something the children were saying or doing. Her eyes were filled with mirth as she swallowed a giggle or chuckle. What a beautiful sight! No one thought of her as funny—and indeed, she couldn't tell a joke. But she enjoyed and was enriched, and that was part of what made her such good company.

STILL MORE CHURCH SIGNS:

God does not believe in atheists therefore atheists do not exist—Palm Heights Baptist Church

Forgive your enemies—it messes with their heads—Donelson View Baptist Church

Free coffee, everlasting life. Yes membership has its privileges—Goodwind United Church

Walmart is not the only saving place—Oak Grove Landmark Missionary Baptist Church

Artificial intelligence is no match for natural stupidity—Neighborhood Christian Center of the Assemblies of God

There are some questions that can't be answered by Google—Claude Presbyterian Church

Work on sensitivity and timing.

During the time I have been working on this book, I have also been studying two solemn subjects—Christianity and the Holocaust, and the Palestinian / Israeli conflict. And since I returned from a summer of study in Israel, there have been horrible earthquakes, hurricanes, floods, wild fires, and an oil spill. Meanwhile, in the world, financial crises come crashing down, one after another, and there is grave concern—individual and corporate about the costs of health care and of caring for the growing aging population.

I must admit that sometimes, when pondering all these things, as well as the individual pain and grief of people I love, my exploration of humor may seem trivial and unfitting. Certainly there are times to be silent or to engage in solemn discussion. If there is humor within any of these, it is for those most affected to claim it, and for me only to acknowledge and affirm.

Still, in the long run, I do not believe such tragedies should or will silence all humor. Indeed, the tragicomedy we explored was born of such times. Perhaps, at such times a little humor is especially needed. We are to heed the wise counsel of the writer of Ecclesiastes that there is a time for every matter under heaven:

A time to weep and a time to laugh;
A time to mourn and a time to dance, (Eccl 3:4)

Find your own voice

And so, when the time is fitting, take steps to find your own voice within the wide variety of humor options. One of my favorite "voices" is the limerick. (Yes, there are clean limericks). I enjoy them tremendously and write them passably. I rarely include them in sermons, but use them in greeting cards, graduation notes to my student advisees, and to "entertain" my long-suffering family.

As we noted in chapter two, there are so many possibilities of humor from which to choose. Experimenting, perhaps feeling awkward with, but stretching and eventually feeling into a style is all part of it.

The important part is not to let someone else's expectation force you into a style of humor that doesn't fit you. A kindly older woman in one of my churches used to give me little scrapbooks of sweet little religious jokes she had clipped from magazines and newspapers, hoping (I guess) to improve my sermons. I enjoyed them, still have one or two, but I rarely or never used anything from them in the pulpit. They just didn't fit me.

You may like puns, or clowning, or jokes, or human interest stories, or limericks, or your choice. Or you may be comfortable with a wide range of these. It needs to be your choice, your comfort level, and your voice.

Find, attend to, and give priority to what renews you and feeds your humorous perspective.

Discover what feeds and sustains you personally. Give yourself permission to give it priority, schedule it, invest in it, and preserve time for it without apology on your appointment calendar. There are many things that can restore and stir up our playful, joyful spirit.

- For some it is time with children or pets or gardens,
- It may be attending concerts, plays, movies, sporting events (an occasional escapist movie sometimes relaxes me and allows my creative juices to stir once more),
- Perhaps it is playing a beloved game or sport,—table tennis, tennis, softball, basketball, soccer, horse shoes—losing yourself in the game for a little while,
- It could be an outdoor activity—hunting, fishing, boating, swimming, white water rafting, camping, gardening, hiking, walking, jogging,
- It might be going to comedy clubs, or collecting humorous books, or DVDs / CDs and enjoying them alone or with friends,
- It could be entering into some art form or craft, or hobby—joining a chorus, trying out for community theatre, playing an instrument alone or with others, drawing, painting, quilting, crocheting, knitting, furniture making, or carving,
- For some, it is time alone—perhaps with a good book—and for others it is getting out among people, being with them, observing them, entering into happenings with them.
- It might be a quiet few moments of relaxation at the beginning or end of the day with a crossword puzzle, word game, Soduku, or bridge column.
- Or, add your own thoughts and possibilities to this list.

Time away from pressures or pain of work to sink oneself in a beloved pastime can sweeten one's spirit and improve one's humor. The problem is that we clergy do this so poorly—both ways. I am aware of two clergy who both loved to play tennis but did so together rarely. One of them almost always had time to play and the other almost never had time for a game.

Wise time management that offers strong pastoral services—balanced by "Sabbath time" whatever that Sabbath includes—needs to be a priority for all who serve. This is urgently true for those struggling to keep a joyous, hopeful perspective against great odds.

Spend time with humorous people

Another door to humor in ministry is to spend time around humorous people. While I told you of three of my humor mentor / friends in the first chapter, I have many "live ones" too, and I hope you do as well. These friendships may be email partners who send good stuff on, family members, old high school, college or military service buddies. Or they may be new friends, discovered in the sharing of interests. All are enjoyable. When you find such friends, cherish them. Spend time together whenever you can. This is a rare and wonderful gift.

Keep a humor journal and a humor collection

Here is a pair of suggestions—(a) keep a "humor journal;" (b) collect whatever entertains you. You may want to do a journal where you occasionally jot things down that strike you as amusing. Since some things are funny only in retrospect, you might want to write down irritating or frustrating things that you can revisit for humor potential later as well.

Collecting humorous materials can be very flexible and fluid. Just a file folder into which to drop funny emails, cartoons, articles or excerpts, one's own budding ideas, and more can be useful. (You may have electronic ways to do this.) One can always throw away things that on later reflection seem too dated or corny to be useful. (I must admit I almost never throw anything away from these.—My wife, Mary Ann, would probably add that I never throw *anything* away, but if she wants to talk about that, let her write her own book.—When I go through these files looking for a particular thing, there are many enjoyable distractions.)

Try the playful suggestions of "experts."

Many books on humor have a chapter on how to increase one's laughter, or playfulness, or ability to make others laugh. Such chapters have numerous suggestions, a few of which might fit a person at any given time. Annette Goodheart has such a chapter, "Twenty-five ways to Help Yourself Laugh." Here are some of her suggestions.

- Smile more, or share your embarrassing moments
- Collect toys (wind-up toys, jacks, jumping ropes, paddleboard with ball on rubber band, jack in the box, etc.)
- Laugh with a baby

"[Gracious Creator] and God of Fools,
Lord of Clowns and Smiling Saints,
I rejoice in this playful prayer that you are a God of laughter and of tears.
Blessed are You, for You have rooted within me the gifts of humor, lightheartedness and mirth.
With jokes and comedy, You cause my heart to sing as laughter is made to flow out of me.
I am grateful that Your Son, Jesus,
who was a this world's master of wit,
daily invites me to be a fool for Your sake,
to embrace the madness
of Your prophets, holy people and saints.
I delight in that holy madness
which becomes the very medicine
to heal the chaos of the cosmos
since it calls each of us
out of the hum-drumness of daily life
into joy, adventure,
and, most of all, into freedom.
I, who am so easily tempted to barter my freedom,
for tiny speckles of honor and power,
am filled with gratitude that Your Son's very life
has reminded me to value only love,
the communion with other persons and with You
and to balance honor with humor.
With circus bands and organ grinders,
with fools, clowns, court-jesters and comics,
with high-spirited angels and saints,
I too join the fun and foolishness of life,
so that Your holy laughter
may ring out to the edges of the universe
Blessed are You, Lord my God
who invites me to be a holy fool. Amen.

(From Hays, *Pray All Ways*, 70–71.)

- Do something out of character
- Tell someone what you laughed about or help someone else laugh
- Have a family reunion with or without your family.
- Do a winking meditation (while staring into someone's eyes in deep meditation)
- Say "Seriously"
- Throw a unique party, perhaps a "slumber party" for adults or something else that touches happy childhood memories
- Buy and carry around a large cuddly teddy bear
- Risk looking foolish, consider a pillow fight
- Play "gigglebelly"—everyone lies on the floor, each person's head on someone else's stomach. Laughter will follow
- Add the words "tee-hee" to just about any statement
- Form a "serious anonymous" group.[22]
- Use your imagination to expand this list.

Decide what fits you and give it priority

As I cautioned, one could easily respond to this list of steps with a sense of frustration and overload. The wisest response, however, will be to pick one or a few things that really appeal and start there. But start. Give some attention to what will nourish you and feed your playful, joyful, hopeful self.

Give whatever you select a high priority. We're in this for the long haul, and this self-care deserves your attention and energy—both for your well-being and those you serve.

Recently I had the joy of celebrating the fiftieth anniversary of my ordination with my seminary and church communities. It brought back vivid memories of that day in my little home church in western South Dakota. My church family provided a banquet—a friendly "roast" really—just before my ordination service. Ward Coull, a witty retired rancher was one of the speakers. His title was "Tools for Ministry." He began, "Richard has feet so big that he has to put his pants on over his

22. Goodheart, *Laughter Therapy*, 125–49.

head." After a few more quips, he concluded, "I guess if Richard wants to be a minister, we better give him some tools to do it." He lifted up a large, well-used, and rusty tool box. I opened it, and crumpled up within it was the beautiful clerical robe the church was giving me! I laughed out loud even as I cried; touched by the lavish gift my small poor beloved church family had sacrificed to give me and the unforgettable way it was presented.

We laughed on my ordination day, and as my friend in the introduction noted, I am "still smiling." For a long time, I didn't know that humor was spiritual or that it was a practice. I just knew I enjoyed it and needed it. But I know it now, claim it, and commend it to you. For we have important work to do.

Two of the things I like doing are laughing and creating. I have enjoyed this journey of researching, reflecting, reminiscing, and writing. This has been fun! It's been good for me, and I hope it is helpful for you. I pray God's rich joy, hope, grace and blessing on you in your life of service. May we all be "on our way rejoicing" (Acts 8:39).

Shalom and Amen.

QUESTIONS FOR PERSONAL AND GROUP REFLECTION

1. Have some of the writings about spiritual disciplines or practices been helpful in your life? If so, which ones, and in what ways?
2. What, from among the varied suggestions for increasing humor in your life are you already doing?
3. What one, two, or three additional things would you like to try to increase your experience of humor?
4. What is your opinion on the author's case for considering humor a spiritual practice? If you are convinced, how are you doing with this practice? What more do you intend to do?
5. How would you assess the amount of stress and strain for today's ministers and church leaders? For you personally?
6. When has humor, your own or someone else's, been helpful and/or redemptive in your leadership and ministry?
7. As we complete this conversation, what are your hopes for your life, leadership, and ministry? What steps—suggested here or elsewhere—can you take to help claim those hopes?

Bibliography

A Prairie Home Companion Pretty Good Joke Book, Introduction by Garrison Keillor. St. Paul: Highbridge, 2001

Adams, Douglas, "Bringing Biblical Humor to Light in Liturgy." *Modern Liturgy*, Volume 6, No. 8.

Adams, Douglas, *Humor in the American Pulpit*. Austin, TX: The Sharing Company, 1975.

Adams, Douglas. *The Prostitute in the Family Tree*. Louisville: Westminster John Knox, 1997.

Allen, Steve. *How to be Funny: Discovering the Comic You*. Amherst, NY: Prometheus, 1998.

Amen, Daniel. *Making a Good Brain Great*. New York: Harmony, 2005.

Anderson, John Louis. *Scandinavian Humor and Other Myths*. Minneapolis: Nordbook, 1986.

Ayers, Alex (ed). *The Wit and Wisdom of Abraham Lincoln*. New York: Meridian, 1992.

Barclay, William. *More New Testament Words*. New York: Harper and Brothers, 1958.

Bass, Dorothy and Don Richter (eds). *Way to Live: Christian Practices for Teens*. Nashville: Upper Room, 2002.

Bass, Dorothy C. (ed).*Practicing Our Faith*. San Francisco: Jossey-Bass, 1997.

Bass, Dorothy, and Susan Briehl (eds). *On Our Way: Christian Practices for Living a Whole Life*. Nashville: Upper Room, 2010.

Baum, Margaret and Loretta LaRoche. "Jest and Joy" in Benson, Herbert and Eileen Stuart (ed).*The Wellness Book*. New York: Birch Lane, 1992.

Benson, Herbert and Eileen Stuart (eds).*The Wellness Book*. New York: Birch Lane, 1992.

Berger, Peter L. *Redeeming Laughter: The Comic Dimension of Human Experience*. New York: Walter De Gruyter, 1997.

Bowe, Barbara. *Biblical Foundations of Spirituality*. Lanham, MD: Sheed & Ward, 2003.

Brown, Robert McAfee. *The Significance of the Church*. Philadelphia: Westminster, 1956.

Buechner, Frederick. *Telling the Truth: The Gospel as Tragedy, Comedy, and Fairy Tale*. New York: Harper and Row, 1977.

Buechner, Frederick. *Wishful Thinking: A Theological ABC*. New York: Harper and Row, 1973.

Buttrick, George Arthur. "God and Laughter," *Sermons Preached in a University Church*. New York: Abingdon, 1959

Buttrick, George Arthur. *Sermons Preached in a University Church*. New York: Abingdon, 1959.

Capps, Donald. *A Time to Laugh: The Religion of Humor*. New York: Continuum, 2005.

Capps, Donald. *Laughter Ever After. . . Ministry of Good Humor.* St. Louis: Chalice, 2008.

Capps, Donald. *Men and Their Religion: Honor, Hope, and Humor.* Harrisburg, PA: Trinity, 2002.

Capps, John and Donald Capps. *You've Got to Be Kidding! How Jokes Can Help You Think*. Chichester, West Sussix, UK: John Wiley and Sons, 2009.

Chapman, Antony and Hugh C.Foot (eds), *It's a Funny Thing, Humor.* Oxford: Pergamen, 1977.

Cohen, Ted. *Jokes: Philosophical Thoughts on Joking Matters.* Chicago: University of Chicago Press, 1999.

Cormier, Henri. *The Humor of Jesus*. New York: Alba House, 1977.

Cosby, Bill. *Cosbyology: Essays and Observations from the Doctor of Comedy.* New York: Hyperion, 2001.

Cousins, Norman. *Anatomy of an illness: As Perceived by the Patient.* New York: McGraw-Hill, 1979.

Cousins, Norman. *Head First: The Biology of Hope.* New York: E.P. Dutton, 1989.

Cox, Harvey. *The Feast of Fools: A Theological Essay on Festivity and Fantasy.* Cambridge: Harvard University Press, 1969.

Culpepper, R. Alan. "Humor and Wit (NT)." *Anchor Bible Dictionary, Vol 3.* New York: Doubleday, 1992.

Darden, Robert. *Jesus Laughed: The Redemptive Power of Humor.* Nashville: Abingdon, 2008.

Dillard, Annie. *Teaching a Stone to Talk.* New York: Harper Perennial, 1982.

Donnelly, Doris. "Divine Folly: Being Religious and the Exercise of Humor," *Theology Today,* Vol. 48, No. 4, January 1992.

Dykstra, Craig. *Growing in the Life of Faith: Education and Christian Practices.* Louisville: Geneva, 1999.

Esar, Evan. *The Humor of Humor.* New York: Horizon, *1952.*

Fasol, Al. *Humor with a Halo: True Funny Stories from Church Life.* Lima OH: C.S.S., 1989.

Feaster, Don. "The Importance of Humor and Clowning in Spirituality and Pastoral Counseling." *Currents in Theology and Mission*, Vol. 25, no. 5, 1998.

Fisher, Eugene. "The Divine Comedy: Humor in the Bible." *Religious Education,* Vol. LXXII, No. 6, Nov.-Dec., 1977.

Foster, Richard. *Celebration of Discipline.* San Francisco: HarperSanFrancisco, 1978, 1988, 1998.

Frankl, Victor. *Man's Search for Meaning.* New York: Washington Square, a Division of Simon & Schuster, 1959.

Freud, Sigmund. *Jokes and Their Relation to the Unconscious*. Repor. Translated by James Strachey. New York: W.W. Norton, 1905, 1960.

Friedman, Hershey H. "Humor in the Hebrew Bible," *Humor: International Journal of Humor Research*, Vol. 13:3, Sept. 2000, 258-285.

Fulghum, Robert. *From Beginning to End: The Rituals of Our Lives.* New York: Ivy Books, 1996.

Garrett, Graeme. *God Matters: Conversations in Theology*. Collegeville, MN: Liturgical Press, 1999.

Geist, Bill. *Way Off the Road: Discovering the Charms of Small Town America.* New York: Broadway Books, 2007.

Goodheart, Annette. *Laughter Therapy: How to Laugh About Everything in Your Life That Isn't Really Funny.* Santa Barbara, CA: Less Stress Press, 1994.

Green, Lila. *Making Sense of Humor: How to Add Joy to Your Life.* Manchester, CT:

Greenstein, Edward L. "Humor and Wit" (OT)." *Anchor Bible Dictionary, Vol. 3.* New York: Doubleday, 1992. (325-333)

Grossman, "The Use of Jokes in Psychotherapy. In Chapman, Antony and Hugh C.Foot (ed), *It's a Funny Thing, Humor.* Oxford: Pergamen, 1977.

Hays, Edward. *Holy Fools & Mad Hatters: A Handbook for Hobbyhorse Holiness.* Leavenworth, KS: Forest of Peace, 1993.

Hays, Edward. *Pray All Ways.* Leavenworth, KS: Forest of Peace, 1981

Holland, Norman. *Laughing: A Psychology of Humor.* Ithica, NY: Cornell University Press, 1982,

Hunt, Harley (ed). *The Stained Glass Fishbowl: Strengthening Clergy Marriages.* Valley Forge, PA: American Baptist Minister's Council, 1990.

Hyers, Conrad. *And God Created Laughter: The Bible as Divine Comedy.* Atlanta: John Knox, 1987.

Hyers, Conrad (ed). *Holy Laughter: Essays on Religion in the Comic Perspective.* New York: Seabury, 1969.

Hyers, Conrad. *The Comic Vision and the Christian Faith: A Celebration of Life and Laughter.* New York: Pilgrim, 1981.

Jones, Douglas M. *The Mantra of Jabez.* Moscow, ID: Canon, 2001.

Jones, L. Gregory and Kevin R. Armstrong. *Resurrecting Excellence: Shaping Faithful Christian Ministry.* Grand Rapids: Wm B. Eerdmans, 2006.

Jones, Loyal and Billy Edd Wheeler. *Hometown Humor, U S. A.* Little Rock: August House, 1991.

Keillor, Garrison. "Gospel Birds: And Other Stories of Lake Wobegon," originally released 1985. Highbridge Audio, 1993. (Compact Disk).

Kidd, Sue Monk. *When the Heart Waits.* San Francisco: HarperSanFrancisco, 1990.

Klein, Allen. *Learning to Laugh When You Feel Like Crying.* NJ: Goodman Beck, 2011

Klein, Allen. *The Courage to Laugh.* New York: Jeremy P. Tarcher / Putnam, 1998.

Klein, Allen. *The Healing Power of Humor.* New York: Jeremy P. Tarcher/Putnam, 1989.

Koppel, Michael S. *Open-Hearted Ministry: Play as Key to Pastoral Leadership.* Minneapolis: Fortress, 2008.

Kuhlman, Thomas L. *Humor and Psychotherapy.* Homewood, Ill: Dorsey Professional, 1984.

Lamott, Anne. *Travelling Mercies: Some Thoughts on Faith.* New York: Pantheon, 1999.

Larson, Bruce. *There's a Lot More to Health Than Not Being Sick.* California: Cathedral, 1991.

"Laughter Yoga as Laughter Therapy." Laughter Yoga International. Online: http://www.laughteryoga.org/index.php?option+com_content&view=article&id=731:laugh.

Leary, James P. *Midwestern Folk Humor: Jokes on Farming, Logging, Religion, and Traditional Ways.* Little Rock: August House, 1991.

Long, Thomas. *The Witness of Preaching.* Louisville: Westminster John Knox, 2005.

Marsh, Charles. "'From the Phraseological to the Real': Lived Theology and the Mysteries of Practice." http://www.practicingourfaith.org.

Marshall, Eric and Stuart Hample, compilers. *Children's Letters to God.* New York: Essandess Special Editions, a Division of Simon & Schuster, 1966.

Martin, James SJ. *Between Heaven and Mirth: Why Joy, Humor and Laughter Are at the Heart of the Spiritual Life.* New York: HarperOne, 2011.

McGhee, Paul E. and Jeffrey H. Goldstein (eds). *Handbook of Humor Research: Applied Studies*. New York: Springer, 1983.

Migliore, Daniel L. "Reappraising Barth's Theology," *Theology Today*, Vol. 43, No. 3, October, 1986.

Mitchell, Kenneth and Herbert Anderson. *All Our Loses, All Our Griefs*. Philadelphia: Westminster, 1983.

Moody, Raymond A., Jr. *Laugh After Laugh: The Healing Power of Humor.* Jacksonville: Headwaters, 1978.

Morris, Danny and Charles Olsen. *Discerning God's Will Together.* Nashville: Upper Room, 1997.

Morseth, Ellen. *Ritual and the Arts in Spiritual Discernment.* Kansas City: Worshipful Work, 1999.

Mullen, Tom. *Laughing Out Loud and Other Religious Experiences.* Waco: Word, 1983.

Newhart, Bob. *I Shouldn't Even Be Doing This! And Other Things That Strike Me as Funny.* New York: Hyperion, 2006.

Niebuhr, Reinhold. "Humor and Faith." *Discerning the Signs of the Times*. New York: Harper and Row, 1946.

Olsen, Charles, and Danny E. Morris. *Discerning God's Will Together.* Nashville, Upper Room, 1997.

Olsen, Charles, and Ellen Morseth. *Selecting Church Leaders: A Practice in Discernment.* Nashville: Upper Room, 2002.

Olsen, Charles. *Transforming Church Boards into Communities of Spiritual Leaders.* Bethesda, MD: Alban, 1995.

Pak, Su Yon, Jung Ha Kim, and Myung Ji Cho. *Singing the Lord's Song in New Land: Korean American Practices of Faith.* Louisville: Westminster John Knox, 2005.

Palmer, Earl F. *The Humor of Jesus*. Regent College Publishing, 2001.

Palmer, Parker. *Let Your Life Speak.* San Francisco: Jossey-Bass, 2000.

Parrott, Bob. *God's Sense of Humor: Where? When? How?* New York: Philosophical Library, 1984.

Patterson, Kerry, Joseph Grenny, Ron McMillan, and Al Switzler. *Crucial Conversations: Tools for Talking When the Stakes are High.* New York: McGraw Hill, 2002.

Peter, Laurence J. *Peter's Quotations: Ideas for Our Times.* New York: William Morrow and Company, 1977.

Provine, Robert R. *Laughter: A Scientific Introduction*. New York: Penguin, 2000.

Regier, Barbara and Leland, "Making Time for Play" in Hunt, Harley (ed). *The Stained Glass Fishbowl: Strengthening Clergy Marriages.* Valley Forge, PA: American Baptist Minister's Council, 1990.

Richter, Don. Personal email 4/17/2008.

Sacks, Oliver. *A Leg To Stand On.* New York: Touchstone, a Division of Simon $ Schuster, 1984.

Salameh, Waleed Anthony. "Humor in Psychotherapy: Past Outlooks, Present Status, and Future Frontiers." From McGhee, Paul E. and Jeffrey H. Goldstein (eds). *Handbook of Humor Research: Applied Studies*. New York: Springer, 1983.

Samra, Cal and Rose. *Holy Humor: A Book of inspirational Wit and Cartoons.* Carmel, NY: Guideposts, 1996.

Samra, Cal and Rose. *More Holy Humor.* Carmel, NY: Guideposts, 1997.

Samra, Cal and Rose. *Rolling In the Aisles*. Colorado Springs: Water Brook, 1999.

Samra, Cal. *The Joyful Christ: The Healing Power of Humor*. San Francisco: Harper and Row, 1985.

Schrag, Paul. "Holy Humor: Sunday after Easter a Time to Bring God's Gift of Laughter to the Sanctuary," *Mennonite Weekly Review*, April 23, 2007, 85th year, No. 17.

Schulz, Charles M. *"Teen-ager" is not a Disease* and *Young Pillars*. Anderson, IN: Warner Press, 1958, 1961.

Schulz, Charles M. *The Lighter Side of Church Life*. Wheaton: Tyndale House, 1988, 1989.

Short, Robert L. *The Gospel According to Peanuts*. Richmond: John Knox, 1964.

Sparks, Susan. *Laugh Your Way to Grace: Reclaiming the Spiritual Power of Humor*. Woodstock, VT: Skylight Paths, 2010.

Swabey, Mary Collins. *Comic Laughter: A Philosophical Essay*. New Haven: Yale University Press, 1961.

Sweet, Leonard. *The Jesus Prescription for a Healthy Life*. Nashville: Abingdon, 1996.

Taylor, Barbara Brown. *An Altar in the World*. New York: HarperOne, 2009.

Taylor, Barbara Brown. *Leaving Church: A Memoir of Faith*. San Francisco: HarperSanFrancisco, 2006.

Taylor, Cheryl, "A Theology of Humor," http://womeninministry.ag.org/0805/0805_Theology_Humor.cfm.

The New Webster's Dictionary of the English Language. New York: Lexicon Publications, 1988.

Thomas, Benjamin P., Edited by Michael Burlingame. *"Lincoln 's Humor" and Other Essays*. Urbana and Chicago: University of Illinois Press, 2002.

Trueblood, Elton. *The Humor of Christ*. New York: Harper, 1964.

Twain, Mark. *The Adventures of Tom Sawyer*. New York: Barnes and Noble, 1876.

Underhill, Evelyn. *Worship*. London: Nisbet & Co. 1936,

Watzlawick, Paul, John Weakland, and Richard Fisch. *Change: Principles of Problem Formation and Problem Resolution*. New York; W. W. Norton, 1974.

Webb, Joseph M. *Comedy and Preaching*. St. Louis: Chalice, 1998.

Webber, William D. "What Do You Do the Day after Easter?" Beliefnet, Daily Inspiration, March 27, 2005.

Weisman, Ze'ev. *Political Satire in the Bible*. Atlanta: Scholars Press, Society of Biblical Literature, 1998.

"What are Christian Practices," http://www.practicingourfaith.com.

Whedbee, J. William. *The Bible and the Comic Vision*. New York: Cambridge University Press, 1998.

White, James F. *Introduction to Preaching*. Nashville: Abingdon, 1980.

Willimon, William H., compiler and editor. *And the Laugh Shall be First*. Nashville: Abingdon, 1986.

Willimon, William H. "Sermon Slips." *The Christian Ministry*. Nov.-Dec., 1988.

Wooten, Patty. *Heart, Humor, and Healing*. Santa Cruz, CA: Jest Press, 1994.

Zeluff, Daniel. *There's Algae in the Baptismal Fount*, Nashville: Abingdon, 1978.